DON'T LET THE KIDS DRINK THE KOOL-AID

DON'T LET THE KIDS DRINK THE KOOL-AID

CONFRONTING THE LEFT'S ASSAULT ON OUR FAMILIES, FAITH, AND FREEDOM

MARYBETH HICKS

Since 1947
REGNERY
PUBLISHING, INC.
An Eagle Publishing Company • Washington, DC

Cataloging-in-Publication data on file with the Library of Congress

ISBN 978-1-59698-151-5

Published in the United States byRegnery Publishing, Inc.
One Massachusetts Avenue, NW
Washington, DC 20001
www.regnery.com

Manufactured in the United States of America

10 9 8 7 6 5 4 3 2 1

Books are available in quantity for promotional or premium use. Write to Director of Special Sales, Regnery Publishing, Inc., One Massachusetts Avenue NW, Washington, DC 20001, for information on discounts and terms or call (202) 216-0600.

Distributed to the trade by:
Perseus Distribution
387 Park Avenue South
New York, NY 10016

For James M. Hicks Jr.
With love and gratitude for a life I never imagined

Contents

Part One:
Undermining Our American Character

Part Two:
How the Left Instill Their Kool-Aid Values

Part Three:
Winning the Hearts and Minds of Our Children

INTRODUCTION

I n 2007, while still a member of the United States Senate, Barack Obama said, "I am absolutely convinced that culture wars are just so '90s. Their days are growing dark." Obama was right. The culture wars are over. We lost.

We are no longer fighting to uphold traditional social values. Now we're fighting a battle over the very definition of what it means to be an American, and what America means to the world. A losing battle.

A decade ago there was talk among conservatives of a strategic retreat. Americans of traditional values should absent themselves from the public square (territory the other side already controlled, anyway), hunker down at home or in private and parochial schools, and raise a new generation of Americans who would grow up to undo the damage the Left was wreaking on all our institutions.

Well, we managed the "retreat" bit, all right. It's the "strategic" part that we failed to pull off. It's easy to see the signs that conservatives, religious people, and patriotic Americans are absent from our entertainment, news media, and public school management.

But is the new generation of American teens and twenty-somethings ready to come raring back and reclaim our public institutions for traditional American values?

In a word, No.

We retreated from the public square. But somehow the Leftism that went unchallenged there managed to follow our children. Home, to their bedrooms, where 70 percent of American kids have their own TV. Onto their computers and cell phones; they spend more than seven hours a day interacting with electronic media. And to their friendly neighborhood public schools, where the dedicated teachers Americans trust with their children's educations are implementing lesson plans designed to make converts for socialism and radical environmentalism.

That's an old story—the "long march" of radical Leftists through our institutions.

The new news is worse. It's not just that Leftists are attempting to instill their radical beliefs in the minds and hearts of children.

It's that our children have swallowed these lessons hook, line, and sinker. Polls prove that on issue after issue, American young people are buying what the Left is selling.

They don't understand the value of the free market. They expect and welcome government interference in the most intimate aspects of their lives. They're sure SUVs are destroying the planet. They're sold on the Left's redefinition of family, and when they reach young adulthood they're failing to form families of their own. They're dropping out of churches in record numbers. They believe Christians are mean and judgmental.

We've been deluding ourselves that in the long run we could win a war of attrition.

After all, we think, conservatives and religious people can actually be bothered to raise children. Homeschoolers, churchgoing Christians, and orthodox Jews still have big families. Liberal atheists stay childless to save the planet (or perhaps because they don't want to grow up themselves).

But the Leftists don't have to have children. They can steal ours.

And to win they don't have to turn our children into angry revolutionaries. They just have to do exactly what they're doing—shape our kids into a generation completely ignorant of the principles that have made America the extraordinary nation it is, and fill them with so much worry over so-called crises (from global warming to the childhood obesity epidemic) that they'll naturally let the government step in and take care of us all. That will be quite sufficient to end the American experiment with republican self-government—in one generation.

Considering our nation's origins, it's obvious why the Left is intent on feeding our kids a steady diet of propaganda. If the path to maintain our republican form of government is to rear citizens who will protect it, then the surest means to devolve into a socialist state is to raise a generation of Americans who will naturally accept such a political system.

They don't do it by promoting a desire for a worker's paradise in our budding young citizens. (Exception: Wisconsin!) Instead, the Left's goal is to inculcate our children with the beliefs, attitudes, and opinions that will predispose them to a socialist America.

In pursuit of their liberal utopia, they are toppling the three-legged stool on which our nation rests: religion, the traditional family, and free market capitalism.

The Left promotes an alternative core belief system—secular progressive collectivism—with all its attendant moral relativism and political correctness.

To truly breed our nation's children into the first generation of American socialists, the Left knows it must manage young America's expectations, creating attitudes of dependence and entitlement. The ultimate manifestation of the socialist worldview is our young people's desire for security over liberty.

Every family in our nation stands at the intersection between politics and parenting, facing a crisis in which the fate of our nation will be decided. But you don't have to be a parent to be concerned. In fact, the result of this campaign to indoctrinate our nation's youth will affect every one of us, regardless of our family status. The reason is simple: our Founders created a nation whose very existence depends upon the virtuous exercise of civic participation by a people who are informed about and committed to the constitutional republic they conceived.

In short, we can't maintain the kind of system our Founders built for us without the kind of people who built it.

The Left knows this. For more than two generations, they have systematically overtaken the most powerful points of access to our nation's children. They're now executing a foolproof plan to socialize our country by socializing its youth.

Indoctrination on our college and university campuses has been well exposed, though it continues unabashed. (Just ask my college daughters how often they've been required to read *The Communist Manifesto*. The U.S. Constitution? Not as often.) And the messages of political correctness, "social justice," anti-capitalism, and moral relativism now permeate virtually every aspect of American childhood.

By the time today's kindergartener reaches college, he will have been served a lifetime of socialist Kool-Aid. This easy-to-swallow liquid is sweet but deadly and may just be fatal to our republic. It's turning our kids into true believers in the Left's agenda—thanks to schools and extra-curricular activities, pop culture and media, and of course, the pervasive presence of government in their daily lives.

Perhaps the easiest way to get American children to drink the Kool-Aid of statism is to appeal to their universal (albeit immature) sense of justice.

We've all heard children moan, "That's not fair!" Parental decisions about bedtime, the consumption of vegetables, curfews, and cell phone minutes will typically elicit a child's assessment of fairness, which in these cases is about the imbalance of power between children and adults.

What really perks up a child's fairness sensor is comparison. Only by comparing one's situation to others is a child truly able to determine what is fair. And just what *is* fair? Having just as much as, or more than, another kid.

A mature person grows to understand that life isn't fair, and that outcomes are the result of circumstances, luck, individual achievement, perseverance, sacrifice—a whole host of factors, many of which are decidedly beyond our control. Inequality of outcomes is inevitable because no two people experience life in exactly the same way. Some enjoy an abundance of opportunities, while others encounter a seemingly endless string of obstacles to success; some squander their blessings with reckless living, others defy their humble beginnings and achieve unimagined wealth and respect.

Ergo, life isn't fair.

It turns out that the propensity to accept inequality in life is measurably a result of age and corresponding maturity. Researchers in Norway released a study in 2010 in which they modified the "dictator game"—a standard experiment used to gauge the development of people's fairness preferences.

In the "dictator game," one player, the "proposer," is charged with dividing the spoils of a game, while other players, "responders," only receive what is given to them. The "dictator game" is really a way for social scientists to observe the decision-making habits of people who are invested with complete power to distribute resources. It's meant to measure the role of economic self-interest versus altruism.

But the Norwegian researchers used it to compare people's sense of fairness across age brackets. And what they found was that adolescents outgrow their willingness to implement an egalitarian (that is, socialist) reward system in favor of one that reflects effort and individual accomplishment. Younger children, when asked to divide the spoils of the game, gave equal shares to everyone regardless of each person's contribution to the outcome. And they didn't mind that some worked harder or were more competent at the game. They naturally practiced "redistributive justice" because it felt more fair.

But the older the children were, the less willing they were to accept equal sharing in the outcome when some had done much more than others to achieve it. In short, older players were okay with unequal outcomes as long as those outcomes reflected actual merit.

The study explains why kids might like socialism. Its focus on equality of outcomes makes sense to a child's limited understanding of justice.

It also explains why socialists like kids. As a belief system—not just a political system—socialism is easily instilled in children. All you have to do is hammer home the notion that competition and inequality, by any definition, are just not fair.

Need proof? Youth sports.

We're now solidly two generations into a culturally accepted philosophy about children and competitive sports that the sporting part is great, but the competition angle is bad. The theory goes that kids don't like to lose (who does?) as it's discouraging and might harm their budding self-esteem. Plus, children can't help it if they aren't equally gifted at a young age in the skills needed for soccer or basketball or football. Better, then, to maintain a system in which everyone is a winner (remember, no one likes to lose!) and all children are rewarded equally for their effort and enthusiasm.

Thus I personally have sat through dozens of youth basketball games in which players and their parents counted the score in their heads because official scoring was not allowed. (Hairy eyeballs to grandpa who boldly pulls out a pad and pencil to track the score. It's just not sporting.)

I'm all for instructional programs for wee ones. After all, children can't compete in a game until they learn to play it properly. But isn't competition also a learned skill? Recognizing that sports are a perfect metaphor for life, don't we want to train up a generation of children who learn to do their level best, work as hard as they can, bring their particular talents and skills to bear, and at the end of the day, exhibit grace in winning and losing?

Don't be ridiculous.

In our new socialist sports mentality, we want to train up a generation of children who learn that everyone is a winner even when they stand mid-field dancing a jig while the rest of the team scurries for the soccer ball. This way, no one is blamed for a loss, because technically, there are no losers. Crucially, every child can *feel* good after such a game, and this is defined as "fair."

Taken to its extreme, you end up with the youth soccer league in Ottawa, Canada, where a rule has been instituted that automatically causes a team to lose if it gets more than five goals ahead of its opponent. That's right, if you go up by more than five goals, you lose. (To avoid this, the league recommends stronger players kick with their weak foot.) Oh, Canada.

But wait…we want to be just like Canada. Don't we?

If only this outcome-based philosophy were limited to sports. The Left always works to "level the playing field" for children, not only in recreation but also in life. In society, this means compensating with egalitarian outcomes for the failure of those the Left deems disadvantaged or oppressed—victims, one and all.

A fixation on victimhood and life's inherent unfairness is central to the appeal of socialism and a key to why it can easily be taught to kids. Compared to concepts such as liberty, self-reliance, self-discipline, self-determination, morality, and equality of opportunity—the principles upon which the Founders formed our system of government—the crusade to institute equality of outcomes fits perfectly with the emotionally immature worldview of a child. For nothing is more childish than the Leftist's battle cry, "That's not fair!"

So will this generation grow out of socialism? After all, in the famous quote sometimes attributed to Churchill, "If you're not a liberal at twenty, you have no heart; if you're not a conservative at forty, you have no brain."

Well, today's children may eventually grow disillusioned with the Leftist Kool-Aid in which they've been steeping all their lives. Reality will certainly mug many of them. Experience, though, is a very expensive teacher. And a slow one. If the next generation reaches adulthood in complete ignorance of the principles America has run on in the past, it may be far into the future before they manage to figure them out again from scratch. Even George Washington, John Adams, and Thomas Jefferson didn't start from zero. They were building on traditional ideas of liberty and timeless virtues that they had inherited from their forbears.

But what's so bad about raising a generation of socialists, anyway? If the goals of socialism supposedly are equality, justice, freedom from oppression, and economic security for all, wouldn't a generation committed to these ideals be resolved to live in harmony with one another and at peace with the world?

Anecdotally, we're already seeing the decay created by this sweetened fruit drink. Today's college graduates tend to be less self-directed, less ambitious, less driven to succeed than were grads even half a generation ago. They expect that they'll have fewer choices and are resigned to making less money, but they don't mind so long as there are "safety nets" to help them along the way.

For example, in my hometown of East Lansing, home of Michigan State University, college students by the thousands use the public assistance "Bridge Card"—an electronic food stamp program—and are encouraged to do so by their professors. In fact, professors apparently make a point of explaining to students how to get the cards, since it's "free money" for students. Nothing like throwing a kegger on the public dime, right?

This is the duplicitous reasoning of the Left. A socialist utopia creates dependent drones. It assures fairness at the expense of freedom; its false security generates a crippling lack of ambition. It offers the phony liberty of a godless, amoral existence, leaving a void of virtue and an invitation to evil.

But this is the ugliest truth of all about the Left's insidious influence over our kids: their pursuit of a socialist agenda not only corrupts our country, it does so by exploiting the innocence, goodness, optimism, and faith of our children.

The elitists of the Leftist political class are foisting a truly hopeless, helpless future on our youngest citizens—using any means to quench their own thirst for power and their desire to dominate those they regard as unenlightened.

Mired in generational public debt, bearing the burden of unsustainable social programs, and forced to obey ridiculous regulations that protect every life form in nature save humans, America's youth have little reason for hope.

Perhaps, being our first generation of American socialists, they won't mind.

I pray, though, that they will.

Standing at the intersection of politics and parenting, I view our nation's future not only as an alarmed conservative American, but also as the mother of four children. I believe they and their generation deserve much more than the hollow, uninspired, unholy existence envisioned for them by the purveyors of pessimism and tyranny on the Left.

In 1775 a great American dad, John Adams, wrote to his wife Abigail, "Liberty once lost is lost forever." The liberty won for us by our Founders was meant for us, but also for the generations that follow us. We're obliged, then, to recommit ourselves to the stewardship of a country whose legacy could too easily be betrayed by our cynicism and indifference.

Adams also said, "Children should be educated and instructed in the principles of freedom." Their citizenship depends upon that education and instruction. Ignorance will be their undoing and our fatal mistake.

We who are lucky enough to be alive in this nation at this time in history now face the responsibility of securing once again "the blessings of liberty for ourselves and our posterity." We face a daunting task, but one worthy of the heirs of the original American patriots—to fight the influence of the Left and instill in the next generation the virtues that will compel them to defend the gift of their American heritage.

Fortunately, that heritage engendered a unique and admirable American character, one that embodies a spirit of optimism and ingenuity, independence and civility, grit and guts, faith and sacrifice, loyalty and love.

It is the birthright of every American child, and our duty to safeguard and bestow.

PART ONE:

UNDERMINING OUR AMERICAN CHARACTER

CHAPTER 1

SKOOL-AID: AMERICA'S LEFTIST SCHOOL CURRICULUM

If your goal were to transform America into a European-style socialist democracy, you would work hard to assure that our nation's youth have very little understanding of our Founders' intentions with respect to American government and civics, and even less appreciation for free market capitalism, the economic system on which our freedom rests.

Success!

A 2009 Rasmussen Report poll measuring respondents' feelings about capitalism versus socialism found that among adults under age thirty, 37 percent favor capitalism as a political and economic system, while 33 percent favor socialism. Roughly 30 percent are undecided. Wow. Nearly two-thirds of young adults don't get that the free market is better than socialism.

And a 2010 report from the Pew Research Center found Millennials—those born after 1980 who came of age around the turn of this century—are the most likely of any generation to self-identify as "liberals." They are "less supportive than their elders of an assertive national security policy and more supportive of a progressive domestic social agenda." (An easier way to describe them would be "Obama supporters.")

Today's college students wear Che Guevera T-shirts because they think the late communist rebel was cool. The idea of Leftist totalitarianism is completely off their collective radar (pun intended). They're convinced it's the *Right* that wants fascism. Their idea of a fearful political enemy isn't communism—after all, America's current generation of young adults grew up in the post-Cold War era; those who, at eighteen, voted for the first time in 2008 were born a year after the Berlin Wall fell—it's terrorism. (But be careful not to say "Islamo-terrorism," as young adults know that's not polite.) If they have any sense at all of our nation's former fervor with respect to communist influences on our soil, they'd likely say it was just McCarthyism, the wacko paranoia of an older generation, depicted in the George Clooney film *Good Night and Good Luck*.

Today's young people aren't remotely fearful of the idea of socialism. Heck, lots of them go to France and Spain and Greece to study abroad and it seems great in those countries, except for the odd (read: regular) rail strikes and the fact that the stores are closed a couple of days a week. And the crumbling European economy. Whatever.

What's causing this political trend? Why do the youngest voters skew farthest Left?

According to a survey commissioned by the Oklahoma Council of Public Affairs in 2009, only 2.8 percent of Oklahoma high school students passed a basic citizenship test. Students were asked ten questions randomly drawn from the U.S. Citizenship and Immigration Services item bank, which includes about one hundred questions. Sample questions were, "What is the supreme law of the land?" "Who is in charge of the executive branch?" and "Who was the first president of the United States?" In the Oklahoma survey, virtually every student failed. Meanwhile, the immigrant success rate for the citizenship test administered around the same time was 92.4 percent.

The results for Oklahoma high schoolers mirror the findings of the Intercollegiate Studies Institute (ISI) about America's college students. In 2006, ISI administered a sixty-question multiple choice exam to fourteen thousand freshmen and seniors at fifty colleges nationwide. The freshmen failed the civic literacy test with an average score of 51.7 percent, while the average senior failed it with a score of 53.2 percent.

In 2007, ISI again tested 14,000 freshmen and seniors at fifty colleges nationwide. This time, the frosh failed with a score of 51.4 percent, while the seniors improved their average score to 54.2 percent. They must have pulled an all nighter.

In 2008, ISI administered a basic thirty-three-question civic literacy test to a random sample of 2,508 American adults. Respondents had a range of educational attainment from high school diplomas to advanced degrees. Questions came from past ISI surveys, as well as from nationally recognized exams such as the U.S. government's citizenship test and the National Assessment of Educational Progress (NAEP) test. Respondents also were asked questions regarding their level of engagement in other activities that may or may not contribute to civic literacy. The average score for all Americans who took this straightforward civic literacy test is 49 percent, or an "F," proving the apple doesn't fall far from the civically illiterate tree.

Despite the fact that America's civic ignorance makes for entertaining editions of Jay Leno's "Jay Walking," in which everyday citizens humiliate themselves by displaying their lack of knowledge (Jay: "What do we celebrate on Independence Day?" Ignorant American: "Ummm...the Fourth of July?"), the fact is, the lack of real knowledge about our history, our government, and our economic system among America's youth is not even a little bit funny.

The NAEP, conducted by the National Center for Education Statistics (NCES), tracks our children's decline in civic learning. Measuring the knowledge and skills required for responsible American citizenship, the study in 2010 found an increase over 2006 in civic literacy in grade four, no significant change (note: no improvement) in grade eight, and a *decrease* in grade twelve in the knowledge of the principles necessary for civic engagement. Not that those fourth graders are hitting it out of the park to begin with—they scored well below the "proficient" range. This means we're literally educating our children from bad to worse.

The NAEP includes a finding that explains the problem: fewer high school students report being taught about the Constitution than in previous years. Only 67 percent reported studying the Constitution in 2010, a five-point drop from 2006, when 72 percent said they studied our founding document. That means a third of high schoolers are not exposed to the Constitution. Just in time to rock the vote.

Given the lack of education in the basic principles of American government and civics, it isn't at all surprising that today's young adults tend toward an especially liberal point of view. And in addition to being civically illiterate, America's young people are demonstrably uneducated about capitalism and free market economies.

You might not draw that conclusion from reading the sunny executive summary of the 2006 NAEP report, the last year for which economics education was assessed. Suffice it to say that the folks at the Department of Education put a positive spin on the fact that 79 percent of twelfth grade students scored at the "basic" level, including 42 percent who scored at the "proficient" level and a scant 3 percent who scored at the "advanced" level. They never mention the 21 percent who apparently don't know even the most elementary things about economics. The headline could have read, "Nearly a quarter of high school seniors lack basic economics education," but then I suppose that would have been snarky. Cheerfully reporting that most students have a "basic" understanding of economics doesn't change the facts, however. On the subject of the national economy, only 36 percent of high school seniors could identify the federal government's primary source of income (that would be taxes, kids), only 33 percent could explain the effect of an increase in real interest rates on consumer borrowing, and a scant 11 percent could analyze how a change in unemployment rates affects income, spending, and production.

It's worth repeating: only about a third of high school students know where the government gets its money. Funny enough, that's almost the exact percentage of young adults that Rasmussen identified as socialist-friendly. I'd argue there's a causal connection, but I'm not a social scientist.

Still, a 2009 Junior Achievement survey found that 51 percent of teens said they would like to someday start their own businesses. (Admittedly, 88 percent of those same teens believe this would be difficult or challenging to do.) That sounds like capitalism is holding on among a slight majority.

Why own a business? Oddly, only 15 percent said they believe this is the path to make the most money, while just 9 percent said owning a business would allow them to create jobs and spur economic growth, and a meager 3 percent said they have a great idea about a new product or service. Most respondents—47 percent—like the idea not because of the contribution they might make to society, but because they wouldn't be stuck working for someone else. It might be that "You can't tell me what to do" now defines our entrepreneurial spirit. Mark my words, those are the folks who one day will work for the government.

Are young people really financially illiterate? The answer isn't hard to determine. Since 1997, a group called the Jump$tart Coalition has documented, through biennial surveys, the overall ignorance of young people on all matters having to do with money and economics. The bad news: financial illiteracy has increased among teens from 42.7 percent in 1997 to an all-time high of 51.7 percent in 2008.

How is it that over half of our young citizens are so uninformed about economics and finance? For starters, guess the number of states in 2009 that required an economics class as part of their high school curriculum. The correct response: twenty-one. The number of states that require testing to determine proficiency in the subject? Just nineteen. (Down from twenty-three in 2007. Not a good trend.)

And as Regina Scotchie, Social Studies Coordinator for the West Virginia Department of Education, noted in 2008 at the third National Summit on Economic Education, simply requiring an economics course isn't sufficient. "The West Virginia Department of Education revisited the vocabulary of economics—which is the biggest problem with teachers, because they do not know how to teach the basics of the subject." Apparently, America's Leftist teacher education programs leave out those pesky fundamentals, too.

The impact of our dismal educational standards where economics is concerned is inescapable. As Tom Horne, Arizona's Superintendent of Public Instruction, said, "I am extremely concerned about the fact that our citizenry is under-educated about basic economics, and this lack of understanding could destroy our economy. *Economic education is a necessary precondition to the very success and future of the United States"* [emphasis added]. Truer words were never spoken, Mr. Horne. But our teachers have another agenda in mind.

America's Kool-Aid Curriculum

If you have ever wondered why your high schooler was assigned to read Barbara Ehrenreich's anti-capitalist screed *Nickel and Dimed: On (Not) Getting By in America* for a high school economics class; or why your middle schooler's math book includes story problems about sweatshops and unfair labor practices; or why your first grader was shown the anti-capitalist video *The Story of Stuff* to learn about the evils of American consumerism, wonder no more.

Our children's educational curriculum has been hijacked by the Left.

Literally millions of middle school and high school students are taught the late Howard Zinn's socialist version of American history, *A People's History of the United States*. Though the book came out in 1980, it continues to gain credibility and popularity—for example, if you peruse course syllabi online, you'll see it's used in many AP U.S. History classes today, probably in part because it's listed as a resource for teachers to consider at College Board's AP Central website. And thanks to Hollywood Leftists such as Matt Damon, who spearheaded a 2009 video version of the book for PBS, *A People's History* has acquired an even wider audience.

Up until his recent death, Howard Zinn actively instructed educators on teaching radicalism in the classroom. In 2008, in a keynote address to the National Council for the Social Studies' annual conference, Zinn told more than four thousand K-12 social studies teachers that they should not teach children to simply pass tests, or worse, to "become sort of another little cog in society's machinery," but to be "imbued with a desire to change the world." How so? By adopting Zinn's anti-American, anti-capitalist, socialist, pacifist mindset, of course.

In pursuit of this aim, Zinn encouraged teachers to "re-examine the premises" on which they taught social studies and history—and to give them up and embrace the realization that American history is best explained by class and race conflict. "One of these [premises] is the idea that we all have a common interest. Everyone in society, that we're one big happy family. That's like the first words of the preamble to the Constitution: 'We the people of the United States.' But of course, we know it wasn't 'we the people of the United States' who established the Constitution, it was fifty-five rich white men in Philadelphia who established the Constitution," Zinn said. (After his hour-long address, the thousands of teachers in attendance each received a free copy of the Zinn Education Project's book *A People's History for the Classroom*.)

To augment Zinn's revisionist anti-American history, the Zinn Education Project offers ready-made lesson plans and multi-media materials for both *A People's History of the United States* and *A Young People's History of the United States* (for middle schoolers and elementary students). Much of this material is free for teachers to download or order online, making it easy and affordable to teach Zinn's famously "alternative" perspective.

Zinn died in 2010, but he left a legacy in the form of two influential and far-reaching Leftist organizations, "Rethinking Schools" and "Teaching for Change." Established in 1986, Rethinking Schools is a radical Leftist educational publisher dedicated to the promotion of a socialist agenda in America's classrooms. Its self-titled magazine was founded by Bob Peterson, Ed.D., who also is founder and a fifth grade teacher at La Escuela Fratney, an "anti-racist, two-way bilingual public school in Milwaukee." He is a former Wisconsin Elementary Teacher of the Year.

Rethinking Schools hopes to improve the quality of education with publications such as *Reading, Writing, and Rising Up: Teaching about Social Justice and the Power of the Written Word; Rethinking Globalization: Teaching for Justice in an Unjust World; Rethinking Columbus* (Expanded Second Edition!); and *The Real Ebonics Debate* ("why teachers need to acknowledge and understand Ebonics in order to teach English more effectively").

It will not come as a surprise that *Rethinking Columbus* is based on Zinn's retelling of the European "invasion" of North America from the perspective of the Arawak Indians, as he did in *A People's History*:

> These Arawaks of the Bahama Islands were much like Indians on the mainland, who were remarkable (European observers were to say again and again) for their hospitality, their belief in sharing. These traits did not stand out in the Europe of the Renaissance, dominated as it was by the religion of popes, the government of kings, the frenzy for money that marked Western civilization and its first messenger to the Americas, Christopher Columbus.

Rethinking Schools' sister organization, Teaching for Change, was founded in 1990 to promote "social and economic justice" through educational materials for teachers and organizational avenues for parents. It claims to draw "direct connections to 'real world' issues...[and] encourages teachers and students to question and re-think the world inside and outside their classrooms, build a more equitable, multicultural society, and become active global citizens." In addition to its web-based resources, Teaching for Change operates a bookstore online as well as the independent, progressive bookstore in Washington, D.C., Busboys and Poets.

These groups have enormous credibility. For example, a signature project of Teaching for Change is *Putting the Movement Back into Civil Rights Teaching*, a collaborative effort with the NEA, PBS, the New England Association of Multicultural Education, Teachers for Social Justice, the D.C. Public Schools, and others. Teaching for Change also partners with Teaching Tolerance and the W.K. Kellogg Foundation.

Teaching Tolerance, founded in 1991, is an outgrowth of the Southern Poverty Law Center (SPLC), a pillar of socialist activism in the name of "social justice." While the SPLC is honorably associated with the Civil Rights Movement in many people's minds, it has other goals besides civil rights. That's why we should read more deeply into the SPLC mission statement, which includes the recognition that "Disparities in academic achievement and educational access demonstrate the need for improved preparation and support for classroom teachers." Great. That's just what we need—more Leftist preparation and support for classroom teachers.

Teaching Tolerance provides free lesson plans and classroom materials and sends its self-titled magazine free to four hundred thousand educators twice annually. Obviously they do a heck of a job. The Association of Educational Publishers honored *Teaching Tolerance* magazine as Periodical of the Year in the Distinguished Achievement Award (adult category) for 2009, one of many awards it has received through the years.

Social Justice Math (Not a Joke)

If history, social studies, and literature are easily hijacked by political Leftism, what about math? Surely, math is safely objective, and therefore unable to be infused with socialist dogma. Right?

Wrong. Rethinking Schools' booklist includes *Rethinking Mathematics: Teaching Social Justice by the Numbers.* And they aren't the only ones pushing socialist math—there's a whole movement devoted to importing Leftism into the study of numbers.

Eric (Rico) Gutstein, a former Chicago public school math teacher who now teaches at the University of Illinois at Chicago, is one of its leaders. A founding member of the Chicago-based Teachers for Social Justice, his 2006 text is called *Reading and Writing the World with Mathematics: Toward a Pedagogy for Social Justice.* Those of us who help our children with math homework may have a hard time understanding the concept of such a book, so here is an excerpt of a review from Britannica Online by British educator Andrew Noyes:

> This is a book about hope; the hope of a better world and the essential role of mathematics in writing that more socially just, future world. It is also a book that challenges teachers to act, just as many of Gutstein's students were encouraged to develop their own sense of social agency. It is also autobiographical and through the ethnographic accounts of the successes and failures experienced en route to developing socially just mathematics pedagogies at Rivera [the Chicago middle school where Gutstein taught], the reader is left in no doubt of both the affordances and constraints that lie ahead for critical mathematics educators.

It bears repeating: this is a math book…about hope.

Is it any wonder America's high school students score abysmally on standardized math tests when their curriculum includes less math and more social justice indoctrination? Especially poor and minority students, who are being used by Leftist educators to advance a political agenda with so-called "urban learning" programs—while their cognitive development languishes. Exactly how is perpetuating the ignorance of urban children going to advance an anti-oppression political agenda?

Teachers looking for more ideas on social justice math need only visit radicalmath.org, a site founded by Jonathan Osler, lead math teacher at El Puente Academy for Peace and Justice in Brooklyn, New York, a "social justice" public high school. (Yes, there is such a thing.)

Osler, who has sponsored symposia on his radical math practices for teachers, declares in his *Guide for Integrating Issues of Social and Economic Justice into Mathematics Curriculum*, "No matter the experiences, advantages, struggles, neighborhood, race, class, and gender of your students, learning math within a social justice framework is important for their understanding of both the math concepts and of their opportunities to be agents of change."

Topics Osler suggests for mathematical consideration include "prisons, racial profiling, the death penalty, poverty, minimum versus living wage, sweatshops, housing, gentrification, homeownership, war, defense budgets, military recruiting, public health, AIDS, asthma, health insurance, educational funding and equity, high stakes testing, class size, environmental racism, pollution, and resource availability." (Excuse me while I Google "asthma as a social justice issue.")

The "benefits" to students of such a curriculum include their ability to "recognize the power of mathematics as an essential tool to understand and potentially change the world...participate in actual (not just theoretical) community service projects and organizing campaigns, and answer the question, 'Why do I have to know this?'"

Good question.

Osler admits the program has some pitfalls. Getting kids ready to take standardized tests is a big one. (Ya think?)

Another is the pesky problem of how to get around the mandated math curriculum—you know, the actual arithmetic, algebra, and so forth that school boards have directed math teachers to impart to their students. In his teacher guide, Osler advises, "Many schools have textbooks that they require their teachers to use. This is both a local and national battle we need to be having with our administrators and officials. You will have to decide on your own if you are willing to teach something other than what you're being told to teach."

To get the social-justice-in-math-class ball rolling, Osler advises talking to students about an issue that interests them. "Young people think a lot along the lines of fair/unfair, so *help them to see what is unfair about the issue you're going to study.* This will also work to get them engaged in the class and the lesson/unit. You can introduce an issue by bringing in guest speakers, showing video clips from movies or documentaries, going on field trips, etc." [emphasis added].

Never one to let the goal of teaching math get in the way of social activism, Osler advises, "It is important not to stray too far from the Unit Question and the social issues, but it is fine to take a few days during the unit to do worksheets or other skill-building activities that you feel will help teach or reinforce the math skills and concepts." A worksheet to teach or reinforce math skills! What a thought!

Hands-on Learning in Legotown

When it comes to imparting radicalism, Leftists don't just talk the talk, they put their politics where their toys are. In December 2006, Hilltop Children's Center, a small, private preschool and child-care provider in Seattle, Washington, made national news for banning Legos. It seemed the five- to nine-year-olds in the after-school program had built a fairly elaborate Legotown, which after several months became a source of conflict and consternation.

According to an article in the progressive education magazine *Rethinking Schools* by teachers Ann Pelo and Kendra Pelojoaquin, negotiations among the children about the distribution and use of "cool pieces" of Legos led the teachers and staff to question the lessons being taught through Lego play. "Into their coffee shops and houses, the children were building their assumptions about ownership and the social power it conveys—assumptions that mirrored those of a class-based, capitalist society—a society that we teachers believe to be unjust and oppressive."

Thus, Legos were banned. Or at least, put away for while, so that the teaching staff at Hilltop could indoctrinate the children into a Leftist belief system that would result in a socialist code of Lego conduct. In fact, this was the teachers' intent:

> We also discussed our beliefs about our role as teachers in raising political issues with young children. We recognized that children are political beings, actively shaping their social and political understandings of ownership and economic equity—whether we interceded or not. We agreed that we want to take part in shaping the children's understandings from a perspective of social justice.

The result? After months of discussions and demonstrations about the evils of private ownership and power, Hilltop created a "community of fairness" about Legos based on three new rules:

- All structures are public structures. Everyone can use all the Lego structures. But only the builder or people who have her or his permission are allowed to change a structure.
- Lego people can be saved only by a "team" of kids, not by individuals.
- All structures will be standard sizes.

Welcome to the People's Republic of Legotown.

The Hilltop story got fleeting attention in the national press—mostly on FOX News and in conservative blogs—as an example of Leftist indoctrination run amok. Since Hilltop is a small private center catering to affluent white liberals (the authors' description, not mine), the impact of this incident may seem insignificant. Heck, given their parents' politics, these kids are probably already learning socialism at home.

Crucially, though, "Why We Banned Legos" was the cover story of a nationally acclaimed magazine for educators. Thousands of teachers subscribe to *Rethinking Schools*, and according to the publication's website, subscribers typically pass the publication on to two or three peers in education when they finish reading it. Thousands more copies are distributed at major conferences for educators and sent to institutions with multiple readers such as school districts, teacher unions, and schools of education.

Thus is the Lego-topia spread from town to town.

The Story of Anti-capitalist Propaganda Disguised as a Documentary for Kids

If your elementary school child bounds off the school bus one day and announces he's no longer going to play with his toys because they're toxic, don't be surprised. He's probably just been forced to watch the alarmist documentary, *The Story of Stuff*.

Written and produced by Annie Leonard, a hard core Leftist with degrees from Barnard College and Cornell University and stints with Greenpeace International and the Global Alliance for Incinerator Alternatives, *The Story of Stuff* uses simplistic animation and sweeping generalizations to "educate" the nation's schoolchildren about anti-capitalism and eco-radicalism. It was funded by the Tides Center (read: George Soros).

Between Youtube and DVD sales to schools and churches, an estimated 10 million people have seen *The Story of Stuff*. It is routinely assigned as part of science and social studies curricula. There's even a faith-based program—*Let There Be...Stuff?*—to inculcate the film's message via religious education classes and Bible study groups. In fact, the dissemination and proliferation of *The Story of Stuff* has spawned a veritable cottage industry of Left-wing cartoons. Leonard followed her smash hit with *The Story of Bottled Water*, *The Story of Cosmetics*, *The Story of Cap and Trade*, and *The Story of Electronics*. And new for 2011: *The Story of Citizens United v. FEC*.

If you haven't seen any of Leonard's films, you must. In fact, I'll wait here while you go fire up the laptop and watch the original *Story*, a 20-minute diatribe that's so misleading and fraught with hyperbole and hysteria that you won't know whether to laugh out loud or yell at the screen.

On second thought, let me save you the trouble. Here are a few gems from the script, delivered in Leonard's smug, serious, and oh-so-expert eco-speak, as she described the materials economy:

The materials economy "is a system in crisis. And the reason it is in crisis is that it is a linear system and we live on a finite plant and you cannot run a linear system on a finite planet indefinitely." (Huh?)

She goes on to explain that "extraction is a fancy word for 'natural resource exploitation,' which is a fancy word for 'trashing the planet.'" She claims, "[In] the past three decades alone, one third of the planet's natural resources have been consumed. Gone."

But there's more: "We are cutting and mining and hauling and trashing the place so fast that we're undermining the planet's very ability for people to live here."

It's worth shouting: this is a video FOR CHILDREN.

After extraction, Leonard tells her mostly-young viewers about the process of producing goods: "So next, the materials move to 'production' and what happens there is we use energy to mix toxic chemicals in with the natural resources to make toxic contaminated products." No qualifiers. Nothing to contextualize the fact that chemicals aren't always toxic (depends on the quantity), or that risk is determined by exposure. Nope. *All* products are contaminated.

But since nasty Americans and our corporations are too selfish to want to look at and smell the "4 billion pounds of toxic chemicals" per year she claims we spew into the environment, Leonard asserts we "move the dirty factories overseas. Pollute someone else's land!" (Never mind the jobs and livelihoods created by global manufacturing and trade. We're just out to pollute other nations.)

Leonard's description of distribution is equally slanted. But nowhere does she vilify the American culture (and thus the people watching her video) more than in her explanation of consumption. "We have become a nation of consumers. Our primary identity has become that of consumer, not mothers, teachers, farmers, but consumers." Clearly Leonard doesn't know any farmers.

Free Teaching Tools Promote the "Stealth Curriculum"

The Story of Stuff is already being viewed in classrooms across America and around the world, but as the film's website puts it, the creators want to "turn up the volume on these issues" in our nation's classrooms. This is why they have partnered with Facing the Future, an organization producing educational resources for teachers and schools.

Facing the Future's mission is nothing short of astonishing: to reach 12.5 million students annually through curriculum resources, teacher workshops, and service learning programs in all fifty states and over one hundred countries by the year 2020. This Leftist group's purpose is undeniably socialist, as conveyed on its website:

> Climate change. Population growth. Poverty. Environmental degradation. Conflict. Global health crises. Intractable global problems? We don't think so. At Facing the Future we believe in the transformative power of widespread, systemic education to improve lives and communities, both locally and globally. Our positive, solutions-based programming is designed by and for teachers, and brings critical thinking about global issues to students in every walk of life.

Thanks to countless organizations like Facing the Future, teachers have seemingly endless resources for indoctrinating America's youth. Free lesson plans, DVDs, course materials, stories, and curriculum guides proliferate like ants at a picnic. But these resources aren't only used by teachers who seek out support for their radical teaching goals; worse, they're used by well-meaning teachers who want interesting, useful, and typically free supplemental materials for the classroom.

In a paper entitled *The Stealth Curriculum: Manipulating America's History Teachers*, Professor Sandra Stotsky, Endowed Chair in Teacher Quality at the University of Arkansas's Department of Education Reform and Chair of the Sadlier Mathematics Advisory Board, wrote that supplemental materials for the subject of history in particular "fly under the radar of historians and other experts with sensitive political antennae":

> The source of the problem with many of the supplemental resources used for history or social studies is the ideological mission of the organizations that create them. Their ostensible goal is to combat intolerance, expand students' knowledge of other cultures, give them other "points of view" on commonly studied historical phenomena, and/or promote "critical thinking." *But their real goal, to judge by an analysis of their materials and the effects they have on teachers, is to influence how children come to understand and think about current social and political issues by bending historical content to those ends. They embed their political agendas in the instructional materials they create so subtly that apolitical teachers are unlikely to spot them.* And they tend to facilitate acceptance of their materials by appealing to teachers' sense of fairness and their presumed obligation to promote "social justice" and withhold negative moral judgments about people or cultures deemed victims of white racism.

In the guise of providing teachers with ideas for a more engaging pedagogy and deeper understanding of a historical phenomenon, frequently one involving instances of prejudice, they recruit unwitting teachers as their agents in cultivating hostility toward America as a country, toward Western culture, and toward Americans of European descent. The poisonous effects of these supplemental resources on teachers' thinking and pedagogical practices can spread throughout the entire school curriculum in the moral and civic vacuum created by neutered textbooks and a host of competing "multiple perspectives." [emphasis added]

Nationalizing the Leftist School Curriculum

Perhaps you heard some encouraging news about something called the Common Core State Standards Initiative (CCSSI), a project of the National Governors Association Center for Best Practices (NGA) and the Council of Chief State School Officers (CCSSO). (American education is a veritable smorgasbord of initialisms. Sorry.)

Launched in 2009 and completed in 2010, the CCSSI is meant to nationalize the academic expectations for America's high school graduates in every state that adopts it. So far, thirty-five states have done so. If you guessed that Texas and Alaska are among the fifteen who have not, give yourself a gold star.

The goal of CCSSI is lofty, indeed:

The Common Core State Standards provide a consistent, clear understanding of what students are expected to learn, so teachers and parents know what they need to do to help them. The standards are designed to be robust and relevant to the real world, reflecting the knowledge and skills that our young people need for success in college and careers. With American students fully prepared for the future, our communities will be best positioned to compete successfully in the global economy.

The name of the game is "college and career ready"—a phrase that Barack Obama and Secretary of Education Arne Duncan repeat so often they must now utter it in their sleep. The problem, of course, is that like most progressive platitudes, this doesn't really mean anything, even though CCSSI has been "validated" by a committee of education experts and adopted by more than half of the country.

Like most everything associated with education reform, CCSSI is largely political. The effort wasn't actually initiated by the NGA or the CCSSO, but by the Bill & Melinda Gates Foundation, which funded it. Bill Gates began investing in American public high schools in 2000 with a small schools initiative.

One of the first recipients of Gates Foundation money to launch a small school program was Rick Ayers. Does that name sound familiar? He's Bill Ayers's brother (and also a draft-dodging Undergrounder who spent ten years on the lam). Rick Ayers was founder of the Community Arts and Sciences small school within Berkley (CA) High, where his students reportedly have taken field trips to places like Mexico and Cuba to learn about social justice. But I digress.

By 2008, Bill and Melinda Gates had to admit that the small schools initiative had failed. No matter how much money they put into the concept, creating small learning environments didn't actually contribute to college readiness in the way the Gates had hoped. Turns out they finally realized that it isn't the size of the school but the competency of the teachers that matters most of all.

Could it be Bill Gates discovered the power of the teachers' union to preserve mediocrity in education?

In any case, he's decided that the best way to impact the effectiveness of "3 million teachers and 27 million less-privileged students" in the United States within fifteen years is to implement national standards for high school graduates. To do this, he's going to spend $354 million on this effort between 2010 and 2014 with the implementation of CCSSI.

Holy cow! That's a great thing, isn't it? Here's the Gates Foundation digging into its deep pockets to improve public education in the United States, and all they have to do is figure out a way to delineate the educational outcomes for *the next generation of American citizens*. (But didn't Bill Gates quit college? Oh, never mind.)

Arguments against this idea are legion, not the least of which is the loss of local control over education that has been the hallmark of American communities since our founding. But perhaps the most compelling argument against CCSSI is that there is no clear definition of "college and career ready," and the standards themselves are essentially empty.

University of Arkansas Professor Sandra Stotsky served on the Validation Committee but was one of five members who did not sign off on the final set of standards (file that under "things the CCSSI website doesn't feature prominently"). In a white paper entitled *The Emperor's New Clothes: National Assessments Based on "College and Career Readiness Standards"* published by the non-partisan Pioneer Institute, Stotsky and co-author Ze'ev Wurman concluded that "No one knows whether Common Core's standards will raise student achievement in all performance categories, simply preserve an unacceptable academic status quo, or actually reduce the percentage of high-achieving high school students in states that adopt them."

Worse, the standards themselves are largely empty. In her letter to Dane Linn of the NGA and Gene Wilhoit of CCSSO explaining her reasons for refusing to validate the standards, Dr. Stotsky explained,

> In my judgment, Common Core's standards for grades 6-12 do not reflect the core knowledge needed for authentic college-level work and do not frame the literary and cultural knowledge one would expect of graduates from an American high school. The standards do require familiarity with foundational U.S. documents in grades 9-12, foundational works in American literature in grades 11-12, and a play by Shakespeare in grade 12, but there is little else with respect to content in lower grades. These minimal requirements, laudatory in themselves, would not be considered adequate to frame a literature and language curriculum in any country.

Dr. Stotsky is one of the only American educators to have written extensively about the issue of best practices for standards development. She led the Massachusetts Department of Education's K-12 standards revisions and has deep experience in the process for creating and validating educational assessments. In her estimation, the process for developing CCSSI "profoundly violated almost all civically appropriate procedures for the development of what would become a major public document."

What, then, was the goal of CCSSI? Clear and simple: it's a power grab to take control of the nation's K-12 educational curriculum and mandate the content and skills that will be taught to the next generation, and the next and the next. And it's mostly empty of specifics because the educational elite doesn't want to codify the Leftist educational agenda that most certainly will be reflected in the curriculum once it is fleshed out.

According to a July 2010 MSNBC.com story,

> The Gates Foundation and Education Secretary Duncan move in apparent lockstep. Two of Duncan's top aides, Chief of Staff Margot Rogers and Assistant Deputy Secretary James H. Shelton III, came from the foundation and were granted waivers by the administration from its revolving-door policy limiting involvement with former employers. Vicki Phillips, who heads the foundation's education programs, and Duncan participated from 2004 to 2007 in the Urban Superintendents Network, a group of a dozen school leaders who met twice a year at weekend retreats co-funded by Gates.
>
> "As a private entity that doesn't answer to voters, Gates can back initiatives that are politically dicey for the Obama administration, such as uniform standards," says Jack Jennings, director of the Center on Education Policy. In the past, states' rights advocates have blocked federal efforts for a national curriculum. Gates "was able to do something the federal government couldn't do," Jennings says.

CHAPTER 2

THE FOUNDATION CRUMBLES: WHAT WAS THE AMERICAN FAMILY

I f the family is the foundation of civil society, America's foundation is crumbling before our eyes. The effects of our disintegrating family structure are evident in the lives of our nation's children. But that disintegration is also irreversibly altering the very fabric of our culture and the structure of our republic.

If that seems like hyperbole, I can only point out that numbers don't lie.

According to a 2010 study from the Pew Research Center, only about half of all adults were married as of 2008. In 1960, that number was 72 percent. Fewer couples are marrying. And marriage itself is becoming a luxury of the wealthy and well-educated. The Pew study indicates there is now a 16 percent gap in marriage rates between college graduates and those with a high school diploma or less; in 1960 that gap was only 4 percent.

And growing numbers of adults say marriage itself is becoming obsolete. In 1978, only 28 percent of registered voters believed the institution of marriage was an outdated idea. Today, nearly 40 percent believe this is so.

Meanwhile, young people report an inclination toward cohabitation without benefit of marriage, and they accept "new" family options. According to the Pew Center, "By emphatic margins, the public does not see marriage as the only path to family formation." Survey respondents were open to definitions of "family" that included unmarried parents and children, single parents and children, and same-sex couples with children. The only scenario that misses the majority definition of "family" is an unmarried couple without kids—proving some conventions aren't entirely lost, though they may soon be meaningless.

If twenty-first-century America still defines a family largely by the presence of children—but not by marriage—we also believe that the erosion of the traditional family is a negative trend. With fully 41 percent of children born out of wedlock as of 2008, including 72 percent of black children, the Pew study found the vast majority of respondents—78 percent—believe growing up with a single parent is more challenging than being raised in a two-parent home. A majority—51 percent—believe that children of same-sex couples face more challenges than those raised in a home built around a traditional marriage.

Sure enough, this isn't just the application of common sense. In fact, research shows, non-traditional families are more fragile and their members are at greater risk.

In 2010, a longitudinal study from Princeton University's Woodrow Wilson School of Public Affairs of five thousand children born between 1998 and 2000 revealed the risks to children born of unmarried parents. "Single mothers and mothers in unstable partnerships," the study found, "engage in harsher parenting practices and fewer literacy activities with their children than stably married mothers. Family instability also reduces children's cognitive test scores and increases aggressive behavior...especially among boys." The Princeton study also found that "welfare programs loom large in the lives of unmarried parents and their children," with mothers who are not cohabiting with or married to the fathers of their children most likely to be receiving benefits at the five-year mark.

One wonders if Woodrow Wilson would be proud. After all, crumbling families mean a larger role for the government in our daily lives.

But if the demise of the family is essential to the expansion of the state, it is far from best for its citizens. Studies show married adults live longer, enjoy better health, have fewer accidents or injuries, experience less depression, and enjoy greater happiness than either single or cohabiting adults. Married men in particular enjoy better health than single men, while married women endure less domestic violence than single or divorced women. And children who grow up in households with their married biological parents achieve vastly superior lifestyles, better health, and greater educational attainment than their peers who grow up in single-parent homes.

Moreover, conventional families aren't just good for the people in them; they're good for society and they protect our freedom. As John Whitehead, founder of the Rutherford Institute, a civil liberties defense organization, explains:

> The loss of the traditional family structure has led to a destabilization in society of "mediating structures"— neighborhoods, families, churches, schools and voluntary associations. When they function as they should, mediating structures limit the growth of the government. But

when these structures break down, society—that is, people—look to mega-structures, such as the state, for help.

Whitehead quotes a study that estimates the public costs of family
breakdown among working class and poor communities exceed
$112 billion a year "as federal, state, and local governments spend
more money on police, prisons, welfare, and court costs, trying to
pick up the pieces of broken families."

But if family breakdown is dysfunctional and costly, and traditional families are such powerful boosters of health and welfare,
why is the traditional family going the way of the dinosaur? Could
it have anything to do with the fact that our media—inarguably one
of the most crucial influences on the attitudes, opinions, expectations, and ideals of our children—relentlessly promotes the idea that
traditional families are obsolete, unnecessary, hypocritical, and even
a little absurd? Conversely, unconventional families tend to be
depicted overwhelmingly positively. Sadly, not only do America's
children experience the daily struggle associated with the demise of
the traditional family, they also see very few examples of healthy,
whole, wholesome families in our entertainment media.

All in the Family—
Twenty-First-Century Edition

Let's stipulate that it's a good thing that the media portrays all
kinds of families. From *Sesame Street* to *Full House*, the *Brady Bunch*
to *Eight is Enough*, *The Parent Trap* to *Terms of Endearment*, television
and movies for generations have displayed the diversity of family
structures that exist throughout our culture. In real life, families
experience death, divorce, remarriage and blending, adoption,

dysfunction, and estrangement, and these situations make for good drama, not to mention easy-to-relate-to comedy.

But since the departure of *The Cosby Show* in 1994 (a show that was strangely criticized—mostly by black activists—as not being a realistic depiction of a black family because the Huxtables were intact, affluent, and highly educated), the trend in portraying family life has been toward single-parent and blended families where sassy tweens talk back to ineffectual adults, and the authority structure in the home is undermined with impeccable comic timing.

Children's shows featuring intact, traditional families are now so unusual that in 2010 Disney launched a new one, *Good Luck Charlie*, to "push a little bit harder on the family-inclusive side of the spectrum" according to Gary Marsh, chief creative officer for Disney Channel Worldwide.

Do depictions of broken or non-traditional families at least portray them as struggling and scraping to get by, since that's what all the research says is true about them? Not necessarily. Who wouldn't want to live *The Suite Life on Deck*, the glamorous Disney existence of brothers Zack and Cody and their divorced lounge-singer mom, who scrapes by but manages to keep her kids in the lap of luxury by working on a cruise ship? That happens all the time. (Note sarcasm.)

Perhaps the reason there are fewer conventional than progressive families portrayed in media is because shows with progressive family models make more money. Yes?

No.

Stephen Winzenburg, communications professor at Grand View College in Des Moines and author of several books on television including *TV's Greatest Sitcoms*, says sitcom cycles, lasting about fifteen years, begin with the introduction of moral characters living in traditional family structures. Over time, plotlines become increasingly progressive and immoral, causing audiences to turn away and ratings to drop. With a resurgence of morality and traditionalism, viewers return. Writing in *USA Today* in 2004, Winzenburg pointed out,

> Most of the comedies being pushed today emphasize rule-breaking and dysfunction without consequence. The Emmy Awards prove that the Hollywood community praises material that breaks taboos without upholding traditional values, such as in *Sex and the City* and *Will & Grace.* Instead, the industry needs to bring back the traditional foundation, in which contemporary issues and characters struggle within a moral culture. Until that happens, the situation-comedy format will remain on its deathbed.

Here's what we know:

- TV can and does promote and encourage specific values;
- The conventional family structure is the most beneficial unit for individuals and for society; and,
- Depictions of such families garner larger audiences and thus greater profit.

These facts suggest one question: Why does the entertainment industry continue to ignore and even belittle traditional families, but promote and glorify unconventional ones?

The short answer: "traditional family" screams "conservative."

Hollywood loves the modern, non-traditional family. Really. The latest show to garner positive reviews and Hollywood buzz is ABC's

Modern Family, a new iteration of unconventional relatives launched in 2010. "10 Dysfunctional TV Families We'd Like to Adopt" on TVsquad.com introduces the fictional Pritchett family:

> Dad Jay tries to be accepting of his adult son Mitchell's gay lover Cameron and adopted Asian baby, Lily, while Mitchell and his sister Claire try to be accepting of divorced Jay's remarriage to the much younger, voluptuous Colombian Gloria, which came with Gloria's wise-beyond-his-years pre-teen son Manny. If we had to point out the most "normal" member of the Pritchett brood, or, at least, the one who puts the most fun in dysfunctional? Definitely Cameron, the flamboyant, flashy-attired boyfriend of Mitchell. He's a Midwestern farm boy who played college football, he collects antique pens, he's a whiz at Japanese flower arranging and he's a classically-trained clown, but the eccentric stay-at-home dad is often the sensitive voice of reason....

It's now a cliché that the gay boyfriend is the show's most likable character.

On the big screen, the summer of 2010 saw the continuing celebration of unconventional families. For example, the Jennifer Aniston romantic comedy *The Switch* found the star playing a single woman who uses donated sperm to impregnate herself. Years later, the good friend whose sperm she unknowingly used (drunken bash, spilled sperm sample, clandestine replacement) appears on the scene, only to discover the uncanny similarities between his neuroses and her son's. Romance ensues.

The formulaic and predictable film likely wouldn't have attracted much notice but for Aniston's assertion that it makes an important point about the current definition of "family." During the film's press tour, when asked if it could be considered selfish for a single woman to bring a child into the world without a father or prominent male figure in his life, the actress was quoted as saying family life has "evolved" from "the traditional stereotype of family."

Leave it to a Hollywood liberal to call society's vision of a family a "stereotype."

Beyond sperm-swap hijinks, Hollywood gave us the Academy Award-nominated *The Kids Are All Right* about a married lesbian couple, each of whom has given birth to a child using donated sperm from the same man. The story follows the family as the teenage children seek out their biological father (whom the lesbian couple only refers to as "sperm donor." You hate men. We get it.).

As you might imagine, given today's Leftist entertainment industry, the film opened to universal acclaim. (No really—that's a category on the movie review site rottentomatoes.com. It actually got "universal acclaim.")

Or almost universal. Two reviewers saw through the obvious propaganda of lesbian filmmaker Lisa Cholodenko, who, with sperm from a donor, gave birth to the child she is raising with her partner, musician Wendy Melvoin.

The *New York Post*'s Andrea Peyser saw the film for what it was—a hatchet job on men:

> The most self-righteously moralistic movie to hit the big screen since *Forrest Gump* preaches an undeniable Hollywood truth: Men, and boys who will be men, are not just bad. They're corrupt, amoral horndogs. And women, especially neurotic, lesbian mommies who drive Volvos, watch gay male porn (go figure!) and get plastered before

lunch, are perfect...this film is set to go down in history as the first major motion picture to make a family led by gay women...seem not just normal, but close to godly.

And Prairie Miller, writing at NewsBlaze.com, aptly noted what is not portrayed in the film:

> Creating the world around them rather than reflecting it, is nothing new in Hollywood movies, and *The Kids Are All Right* is no exception. A contradictory mix of a same sex nontraditional family and traditional family values, this married lesbians with kids dramedy seems to want to have its conservative cake and eat it liberally too. Meanwhile, all sorts of elephants in the room having to do with the conflicts and stresses experienced by gays in the first place or by those being raised by them, get the strictly silent treatment....

Silent treatment indeed. Writer and director Cholodenko wasn't likely to include the truth about the problems faced by the offspring of sperm donation. But since she herself is raising a child via sperm donor, she may want to read the research from the Commission on Parenthood's Future, a non-profit that studies the impact of nontraditional parenting.

In the groundbreaking report *My Daddy's Name is Donor: A New Study of Young Adults Conceived through Sperm Donation*, scholars found that the offspring of donors "fare worse than their peers raised by biological parents on important outcomes such as depression, delinquency, and substance abuse."

Moreover, the study reported that, of the children themselves,

- Two-thirds agree, "My sperm donor is half of who I am";
- About half are disturbed that money was involved in their conception;
- More than half say that when they see someone who resembles them they wonder if they are related;
- Nearly half say they have feared being attracted to or having sexual relations with someone to whom they are unknowingly related;
- Two-thirds affirm the right of donor offspring to know the truth about their origins; and
- About half of donor offspring have concerns about or serious objections to donor conception itself, even when parents tell their children the truth.

Of course, Hollywood can always just slap on a happy ending—something you can't count on in real life.

Am I suggesting that entertainment media has singlehandedly caused the high rates of divorce and unmarried parenthood that have plagued our nation for generations? Or that Hollywood Leftists alone are leading the charge for gay marriage and gay adoption? Of course not.

But does entertainment media marginalize the traditional family, and thus contribute to its decline? You bet, and this is entirely by design. In his 2011 bombshell book *Primetime Propaganda*, author Ben Shapiro relays first-hand accounts of radical Leftists who deliberately use their positions of power and influence, as well as their access to the public airwaves, to both promote radicalism and put down conservatives and their values. The fact that it's happening is no longer a dirty little secret, but a point of pride for progressives in Hollywood.

Normal Is Relative
(and Not Always Normal)

Remember the scene in Disney's *Beauty and the Beast* where Belle and Beast waltz around the castle ballroom while Mrs. Potts sings the movie's beautiful theme song?

I'll bet you didn't know that scene *imposes* a heterosexual identity on our kids. That's according to Karin A. Martin and Emily Kazyak, two researchers from the University of Michigan who in 2009 determined that Disney movies construct "hetero-romantic" love and "heterosexiness," and thereby promote "heteronormativity" in children's media. According to the article's abstract, "the authors suggest heterosexual exceptionalism may extend the pervasiveness of heterosexuality and serve as a means of inviting investment in it."

In other words, the University of Michigan research team thinks Disney movies are unfairly biased against homosexuality and—shock! horror!—make heterosexuality seem both normal and appealing. Disney, according to Martin and Kazyak, depicts hetero relationships as "exceptional, powerful, magical, and transformative," and portrays men as "gazing desirously at women's bodies."

My inclination is to point out that this rubbish emanates from Ann Arbor, so what else can we expect? (Full disclosure: I'm a Michigan State University graduate.) On the other hand, there are plenty of people in Hollywood thinking along similar lines. One need watch only an episode or two of the FOX hit *Glee* to see how this agenda is advanced. Ryan Murphy, *Glee*'s brilliant creator and director, is an outspoken gay activist who uses his creative platform to question the concept of heternormativity in storylines about teens. Sometimes the teens turn out to be straight, but as often as not they're gay or bisexual, and that's portrayed as extremely positive.

Not all Hollywood activists are gay, but many are on Out.com's "4th Annual Power 50," a list of power-brokers in media, business, advocacy, and politics that includes Ellen DeGeneres, Adam Lambert, Neil Patrick Harris, Disney chief executive Rich Ross, producer Scott Rudin, and media mogul David Geffen, among others. They view their values about sex and families as both progressive and positive, and they infuse those values into their work.

And in case these creative and energetic people should flag in their efforts to redefine the American family, well-established advocacy groups are on the spot to push the same agenda. The Gay Lesbian Alliance Against Defamation (GLAAD) and The Media Project aggressively consult with studios and production companies to incorporate their political and cultural agendas into the story lines of popular TV shows.

GLAAD tracks its success with an annual report, *Where We Are On TV*. In the 2009-2010 season, GLAAD celebrated that "lesbian, gay, bisexual and transgender (LGBT) representations have increased slightly for the second year in a row" in scripted prime time broadcast television shows, accounting for 3 percent of all scripted regular characters. This was up from 2.6 percent in 2008 and 1.1 percent in 2007. The winning network is ABC with 5 percent.

Those percentages are so small you're led to believe the impact isn't great. But GLAAD doesn't weight their character count for audience share, and gay characters are on some of the most popular shows on TV, reaching some of the widest audiences. For example, in 2008, a record twenty-two series on ABC, NBC, CBS, FOX, and CW featured a total of thirty-five LGBT characters. This didn't include reality shows like Showtime's *The L Word*.

GLAAD's agenda is obvious. More insidious is the influence of the Media Project.

For more than twenty years this arm of the Los Angeles-based Advocates for Youth has "worked with the entertainment industry to place sexual health information and responsible sexual health images on television." On its website, the Media Project brags that it has been "directly responsible for helping the industry to include accurate sexual health content and relevant story lines into more than 40 episodes of various popular television shows, reaching well over 30 million Americans." The mission statement of its parent organization reads, "Established in 1980 as the Center for Population Options, Advocates for Youth champions efforts to help young people make informed and responsible decisions about their reproductive and sexual health. Advocates believes it can best serve the field by boldly advocating for a more positive and realistic approach to adolescent sexual health."

That sounds innocuous, doesn't it? Who could possibly object to "health," to "informed" and "responsible" decisions, or to taking a "positive," "realistic," and "accurate" approach?

How does the Media Project work toward these goals? By fighting abstinence education; promoting adolescents' right to sexual health services without their parents having any say in the matter, or even being informed if their teens are having sex, going on birth control, or being referred for abortions; and infusing entertainment media with "realistic" (that is, values-free) images of adolescent sexuality.

While the Media Project applauds itself for successfully incorporating "accurate" and "relevant" information about sexual health into our TV programming, a Kaiser Family Foundation (KFF) study found that the sexual content of television was increasing while the percentage of television shows that incorporate messages about sexual risk and responsibility has stagnated for a decade. The real-life consequences of sexual behavior are apparently not a part of the Media Project's "realistic" approach to the subject.

The KFF's longitudinal study, *Sex on TV 4*, found that between 1997 and 2005 the percentage of programs that include sexual content increased by 10 percent; the proportion of programs that presented talk about sex increased 12 percent; and programs that actually portrayed sexual behavior increased 14 percent (including 11 percent depicting sexual intercourse), all statistically significant changes. Meanwhile, depictions of sexual risk and responsibility have remained the same, at about 10 percent.

Importantly, KFF also measured the prevalence of "sexual patience" on TV. They found examples in just 1 percent of the programming they evaluated. It's fair to say the folks who produce TV shows don't think much of self-control as a plot device, much less a beneficial habit to be promoted.

They also don't appear to think much of marriage. A 2008 Parents Television Council (PTC) study examined all scripted prime time entertainment programs and found the idea of sex within the context of marriage depicted almost not at all, while sex outside of marriage—as well as every conceivable kinky sexual practice and proclivity—was widely discussed and depicted. And in studies from the American Academy of Pediatrics (AAP), it's been established that our media is the most sexualized in the Western hemisphere, and that adolescents' "sexual media diet" is predictive and indicative of sexual behavior.

Knowing these facts makes it even more disturbing to grab the remote and click over to MTV on a Monday night at 10 p.m. Eastern time to watch an episode of *The Hard Times of RJ Berger*, a "teen sex comedy" about a nerdy fifteen-year-old whose claim to fame is a notoriously large penis.

I've joked through the years that MTV is destroying civilization as we know it, what with its penchant for infecting the minds of our youth with shows like *Real World, The Osbournes,* and *Laguna Beach: The Real Orange County*, not to mention the annual romp through reality known as *Spring Break*. But then in 2010, the network gave us the ethnic-Italian reality show *Jersey Shore* and I realized it wasn't a joke. MTV *is* killing the culture. Its 2011 effort to corrupt our youth is *Skins*, a show so full of out-of-control sexual behavior that the PTC calls it the most dangerous program on TV.

But unfortunately, sexual content for young audiences isn't limited to the MTV network. The AAP estimated that the average young TV viewer was exposed to fourteen thousand sexual references each year—in 2001!

Beyond promoting extremely permissive ideas about teen sex, today's Hollywood elites support the Left's campaign to normalize homosexuality. Ever since the likable and funny Ellen DeGeneres outed herself on her sitcom *Ellen* in 1997, gay characters have gradually become mainstream in scripted entertainment, especially in shows targeted to young viewers.

"Sex and Socialism Sitting in a Tree..."

It's almost surreal how the Left has persuaded Americans over the past fifty years that traditional families and sexual mores are old fashioned and unrealistic. The values baby boomers learned about sex and families in the second half of the twentieth century were generally similar to those held by our Founders. But the values of children growing up today are radically different. Reflected in our popular culture, it's the contrast between *The Waltons*, the classic 1970s show about a multi-generational family in Depression-era West Virginia, and *Modern Family*, the twenty-first-century iteration that puts the "fun" in dysfunctional.

Yet the campaign against traditional ideas about sex and families goes back long before the sixties sexual revolution, the seventies feminist movement, the gay rights activism of the eighties, or the vapid content of twenty-first-century primetime TV. Disdain for the traditional family lies at the very heart of socialism as envisioned by Karl Marx. In his eyes, heterosexual marriage facilitated the oppression of women, the accumulation of wealth and property, the enslavement of children, and the sexual repression of everyone.

Leftist radicals were the earliest proponents of gay rights. In the early twentieth century, activist Harry Hay, a card-carrying Communist, became the father of the American gay rights movement. (Trivia: Hay's lover was Grandpa Walton, Will Geer. Weird, I know.) In fact, former Obama administration "safe schools" czar Kevin Jennings is known to invoke the influence of Harry Hay as an inspirational gay rights leader for our time. Many gay rights leaders of today are strident Leftists who believe the status of LGBT people constitutes political oppression and is part of the class struggle that includes women, the poor, minorities, immigrants, and workers.

Undoing the Judeo-Christian model of the family by dismantling the very essence of what it means to be a man or woman, and instead reducing us to mere sexual animals who create and recreate social "bands"—like wild ponies—is a cornerstone of the socialist world-view that reduces human beings to a lowest common denominator.

Our nation is moving in this direction because there's Kool-Aid everywhere, especially in the movies and TV shows aimed at our children, as well as the songs they hum mindlessly while doing homework. The Left has access to our children through our entertainment media. They're using that access to transmit a strong, unified, cohesive message that the traditional American family is a thing of the past.

Shame on us if we're surprised by the outcome.

CHAPTER 3

HEAVEN FORBID: THE LEFT'S CAMPAIGN AGAINST GOD

When historians one day look back on the rise and fall of the American Republic, it won't only be our habitual deficit spending and lack of financial discipline they blame for our demise, but the deficit of faith and lack of religion in our children's generation. The beliefs and values that once served as the foundation for our government and the moral compass for our society already have been so undermined among our youth that it may take a miracle to restore them.

The Bible says nothing is impossible with God. The spiritual revival we need may test that theory.

"Young Americans are dropping out of religion at an alarming rate of five to six times the historic rate (30 to 40 percent have no religion today, versus 5 to 10 percent a generation ago)." That's the conclusion of "top political scientists Robert Putnam and

David Campbell," presenting research from their book *American Grace* at the May 2009 Pew Forum on Religion and Public Life, according to a 2010 *Christianity Today* article.

Non-belief among young Americans is growing. In a 2009 survey, 22 percent of eighteen- to twenty-nine-year-olds claimed "none" when asked about their religious affiliation—double the 11 percent in 1990.

Respect for Christianity in particular has seen a decline among young people. In a 2007 study of teens and young adults, the Christian research firm The Barna Group found that sixteen- to twenty-nine-year-olds were "more skeptical of and resistant to Christianity than were people of the same age just a decade ago."

Perceptions of Christianity among young non-Christians include "that present-day Christianity is judgmental (87%), hypocritical (85%), old-fashioned (78%), and too involved in politics (75%).... The most common favorable perceptions were that Christianity teaches the same basic ideas as other religions (82%), has good values and principles (76%), is friendly (71%), and is a faith they respect (55%)."

But these negative perceptions aren't limited to non-Christians. The study found that even *Christian* teens and young adults held these opinions. "Half of young churchgoers said they perceive Christianity to be judgmental, hypocritical, and too political. One-third said it was old-fashioned and out of touch with reality."

Rather than espouse traditional Christianity, America's youth essentially have grown into a generation of unchurched Universalists. In *Soul Searching: The Religious and Spiritual Lives of American Teenagers,* Professors Christian Smith and Melinda Denton analyzed the National Study on Youth and Religion to identify the predominant belief system of American teens as "Moralistic Therapeutic Deism." Its five basic tenets are that:

- God is distant;
- God wants people to be nice to each other;
- God wants us to be happy above all else;
- God helps us when we have problems; and,
- Being a good person is the measure of one's life.

This religion has no use for sin, suffering, sacrifice, or salvation. And it certainly does not reflect the religious or moral conviction that inspired our Founders to seek a home for religious freedom.

How did we go from a predominantly Christian, churchgoing nation to a country of lukewarm, vaguely spiritual young people in only two generations?

First, we have to acknowledge that the Left would have to eradicate God from our culture in order to achieve their progressive purposes. God and progressivism are mutually exclusive. Without God, man is free to break or even rewrite the moral law as he sees fit, and he is solely responsible for correcting the "injustices" and imperfections of the world in which we live. Without God, government becomes the ultimate source of creation, morality, and truth.

Now if you wanted to eliminate God from a society, it seems like the first thing you'd do is get rid of the churches. (Funny how nefarious Leftism is so easy to follow!) Sure enough, the most insidious and dangerous way in which religious belief among our children has been undermined is through endless servings of "diversity." Under the guise of promoting tolerance, children are taught that all religions are essentially the same—including the "religion" of atheism. By watering down differences among faiths and equating them all with secular humanism, the Left is succeeding in eliminating religious conviction.

Of course, this stuff looks open-minded and big-hearted when they serve it up. Remember the part of President Obama's inaugural address when he went out of his way to describe us as "a nation of Christians and Muslims, Jews and Hindus, and non-believers." Under the guise of inclusiveness, the president deftly elevated atheism to the status of one of the world's great religions.

Pretty sly, and alarmingly effective.

But it's more than just the blurring of distinctions between religious beliefs and irreligion. As we'll see, the radical Left has used every avenue of entry into the hearts and minds of our nation's children to eliminate faith in God as the source of moral authority. Into this void, they've crammed the secular religion of socialism, developing in an entire generation a belief system that elevates government to the role of arbiter of justice and provider of all that is good.

Since belief in God enables people to resist the tyranny of socialism, it makes sense that the Left has worked to eliminate this crucial barrier to its vision of a statist utopia. The relentless effort to delete all evidence of religion from the public square and our public schools is only surpassed by the cynical and offensive manner in which God and faith are portrayed in the media. That's a very effective one-two punch.

It's Not Just Prayer They've Banned; It's God

The mere mention of God seems to prompt school officials to put their schools on intellectual and spiritual lock down. In the past few years, cases like these have become commonplace:

- A fifth grade Pennsylvania girl was barred from passing out fliers inviting her classmates to a Christmas party at her church, even though she did so during non-instructional time and the party was being held off school property and outside of school hours, and despite the fact that other students are permitted to distribute invitations and fliers for private parties and community events. She had fallen afoul of an unconstitutional school district policy that "prohibits any student expression, written or verbal, that promotes Christianity or a religious point of view."

- Cheerleaders at Lakeview-Fort Oglethorpe High School in north Georgia were ordered to stop the years-long practice of creating banners painted with inspirational phrases, including biblical verses, through which their football team ran onto the field before games. Based on an overly broad interpretation of the Constitution's Establishment Clause claiming uniformed cheerleaders represented the high school, and therefore the government, school officials determined the team could only run through innocuous, unreligious phrases like, "This is Big Red Country." Despite the fact that the cheer team paid for the signs themselves, and that they were not asked by the school to paint and hold the signs (they did so of their own volition), they were allowed to post their banners only several yards outside the football stadium in a "designated free speech zone." (Silly me. I thought that was the entire United States of America under the First Amendment.)

- Raymond Hosier, of Schenectady, New York, sued his middle school for repeatedly suspending him for wearing rosary beads around his neck to school. Applying the Schenectady City School District's policy against gang-related attire, officials barred Hosier from wearing the rosary, claiming rosaries are sometimes associated with gang symbols. Hosier, a devout Catholic, wore the beads in remembrance of his brother, who died in a bike accident and was holding the beads at the time of his death. A federal judge ultimately ordered Hosier reinstated at the school and upheld his right to wear a rosary.

- A Tomah Area High School student in Madison, Wisconsin, sued his school district after being told to remove a religious reference in a piece of artwork he created for a class. The school's grading policy banned depictions of "blood, violence, sexual connotations, [or] religious beliefs," though students whose work portrayed demon-like creatures were not censored. Only after a court hearing did the district negotiate a settlement in which the student's work would be graded and all references to disciplinary action that had been taken against him would be removed from his records.

In the spring of 2011, an elementary school in Seattle actually required students to use the term "spring spheres" instead of "Easter eggs"—proving that the quest to secularize our children has gone from serious to ridiculous.

The rights of teachers to freely express their religious views are also under attack. For example, the Poway Unified School District in San Diego forced long-time math teacher Brad Johnson to take down classroom banners with common phrases like, "In God We Trust," "One Nation Under God," "God Bless America," and "God Shed His Grace on Thee."

According to the Thomas More Law Center, which represented Johnson, his banners had hung for some twenty years without complaint. In addition, the school district allowed other displays of religious references or messages, including "a 35 to 40 foot string of Tibetan prayer flags with images of Buddha; a poster with the lyrics from John Lennon's anti-religion song 'Imagine,' which begins, 'Imagine there's no Heaven'; a poster with Hindu leader Mahatma Gandhi's '7 Social Sins'; a poster of Muslim leader Malcolm X; and a poster of Buddhist leader Dalai Lama." The selective violation of Johnson's free speech and religious expression was so obvious that even the notoriously liberal U.S. Court of Appeals for the Ninth Circuit found in his favor.

Often, it's not a school district but the American Civil Liberties Union (ACLU) that either seeks out willing plaintiffs or simply takes offense on behalf of no one in particular to eradicate any semblance of religion from the lives of America's youth. No organization is more dedicated than the ACLU to working for the sanitized secularization of American childhood.

For example, in Enfield, Connecticut, the school district was forced by an ACLU lawsuit to move its graduation ceremonies from a local Christian megachurch where commencement exercises had been held for several years. The district rented the church because of its ample seating, parking, handicapped accessibility, and safety.

For months, while the ACLU and its litigation partner, Americans United for the Separation of Church and State (AU), threatened legal action, the school board sought alternative sites for graduation. Finally, after an exhaustive search for a location that would accommodate the expected number of attendees with appropriate amenities at a price the district could afford, the board determined that First Cathedral remained its best option.

Following through on its threat, the ACLU sued, and easily found a federal judge who shared its desire to eradicate all suggestions of religion—even those that are obviously inadvertent—from every public event. In a legal opinion betraying a certain paranoia about religion, U.S. District Judge Janet Hall agreed with the ACLU, saying, "By choosing to hold graduations at First Cathedral, [the district sends] the message that it is closely linked with First Cathedral and its religious mission, that it favors the religious over the irreligious and that it prefers Christians over those that subscribe to other faiths, or no faith at all." A thorough study of school board transcripts sends a different message—that the district is closely linked with handicapped parking spots and cheap rental fees.

It's no wonder school boards don't know how to operate in what feels like a pro-atheist, anti-religious culture; the threat of ACLU lawsuits, along with a general misunderstanding of the Constitution, cause well-intentioned school administrators and school board leaders to adopt ill-advised—and sometimes unconstitutional—policies.

But the drive to expel God from the schoolyard has morphed into a campaign to exorcise him from the hearts of the people who play there. And that's not the fault of well-meaning school board members or overzealous superintendents. It's evidence of an orchestrated effort on the part of a growing, militant anti-theist movement. Along with the ACLU and the AU, groups like the American Humanist Association (AHA), the Secular Coalition for America, and especially American Atheists—perhaps the most ardently anti-religious organization of them all—are on a mission to secularize our nation.

American Atheists was founded in 1963 by Madalyn Murray O'Hair, the activist whose lawsuit, *Murray v. Curlett*, helped to abolish prayer in America's public schools. The organization claims to be the "premier atheist organization laboring for the civil liberties of Atheists, and the total, absolute separation of government and religion." But the goals of American Atheists are larger than just separating government from religion. According to its website, the organization opposes school prayer not only because "secular institutions like the public schools should NOT be a forum for religious ritual or indoctrination," but also because "prayer is not efficacious. School prayer is obviously a form of religious indoctrination; it teaches children that there are invisible, supernatural entities which can be implored and appeased through mumbling prayers or reading from holy books." Respect for the views of others? Not so much.

Some atheists like the renowned Richard Dawkins actually are anti-theists, whose goal is to spread non-belief as empirical truth. Dawkins and other radical Leftists don't only want the freedom to be non-believers, or the secularization of public schools and the public square. They are out to undermine and deconstruct the religious convictions of children on the grounds that such beliefs are both wrong and harmful.

Indeed, Dawkins asserts that teaching children religious dogma constitutes child abuse comparable to physical or sexual abuse on the part of religious leaders: "If you can sue for the long-term mental damage caused by *physical* child abuse, why should you not sue for the long-term mental damage caused by *mental* child abuse? Only a minority of priests abuse the bodies of the children in their care. But how many priests abuse their minds? Why aren't Catholics and ex-Catholics lining up to sue the church into the ground, for a lifetime of psychological damage?"

Atheists and church-state separation absolutists aren't exactly friendly to Bible studies and religious clubs in public schools. They use lawsuits to drive religious expression into the private sphere because they want the public square to be value-neutral ground, where people of all religious faiths—or none—can meet on equal terms, right? Wrong. Based on their behavior, it's clear atheists don't want the schools and other public forums to be neutral territory. They want to win that ground for irreligion.

If only anti-theists could form clubs at schools…then they'd have a better shot at undermining religious indoctrination. Enter the Secular Student Association (SSA), whose mission is to "organize, unite, educate, and serve students and student communities that promote the ideals of scientific and critical inquiry, democracy, secularism, and human-based ethics." SSA insists it only seeks to provide the same peer support for college and high school students as do comparable religious clubs.

Boasting a growing list of more than 250 affiliated college and university chapters, SSA now has set its sights on infiltrating America's high schools. Its slogan, "Mobilizing Students for a New Enlightenment" reveals that SSA clearly means to do more than simply support students who don't believe in God. They're looking to advocate for anti-theism.

In a blog post at atheismresource.com, SSA Campus Organizer and High School Specialist J. T. Eberhard reveals, "All reliable polling indicates that atheism is gaining ground in every age group, but the demographic in which we're making the most rapid progress is in young people. This [*USA Today* article] is getting some peoples' attention (read the comments and watch religious people freaking the f—out) and causing those of us advocating for their rights to develop new strategies to overcome new hurdles."

As you might expect, the *USA Today* article to which Eberhard refers sympathetically highlighted the plight of atheist students, equating their struggles to "come out" and be accepted for who they are with those of gay students. "Godless teens want the same social benefits that evangelical teens find at the annual 'See you at the pole' flagpole prayer events at thousands of schools every September, and the court-sanctioned after school Bible clubs, and Christian, Jewish and Muslim student groups," wrote author Cathy Lynn Grossman.

Eberhard also invokes the Left's familiar victim status as a reason to promote high school-based SSA chapters, because, well, claiming you're a victim of bullying works. "We have multiple leaders of high school groups who must lead secretly for fear of retaliation. We cannot so much as send them packages with their names on them. Atheist students are bullied and isolated. High school is a tough time for anybody, especially atheists. Atheist clubs/groups provide an outlet for all the closeted atheists to have the same social opportunities and refuge from bullying and harassment available to every other student."

Praising the courage of a young atheist student to organize a high school SSA chapter, Eberhard reveals his true agenda: "More and more young people are coming out and refusing to be marginalized. These students are the future of our country. They are fearless, dedicated, and they are *casting away the shackles of religion in greatly increasing numbers*. The future is brighter than it's ever been" [emphasis added].

So despite claiming that SSA has "nothing in our mission statement about tearing down religion," Eberhard believes religion "shackles" young people in belief systems which should be "cast off." Thanks to the efforts of the ACLU, the SSA, and other secular activist groups, America's children are learning an entirely backward interpretation of separation of church and state—not that we are freely religious, but that our nation is meant to be religion-free.

Your Religion Is a Joke
(Especially If You're a Christian)

At the same time America's youth learn that God is not "appropriate" in the public spaces of their daily lives, they also absorb the Left's anti-theist bias through the popular culture.

In American pop culture, no one has a larger or more powerful platform to express his anti-religious bigotry than Seth MacFarlane, creator of the FOX network's hit shows, *Family Guy, American Dad,* and *The Cleveland Show*. An outspoken and abrasive atheist, MacFarlane holds religion in contempt and believes, as he shared with fellow atheist activist Bill Maher, it's about time atheism came into its own. Here's the conversation the two had on Maher's HBO *Real Time* in May 2009:

> MAHER: And you are an atheist?
>
> MACFARLANE: I am. Yep.
>
> MAHER: And what do you think of the fact that it's a movement that seems to be gaining credibility of late?
>
> MACFARLANE: I think it's about f—ing time.… I think you saw people who had eight years of being told nothing other than "Love Jesus and you'll be fine," you know 9-11 and Jesus.… And they're finally starting to come out of that and realizing that maybe if he's wrong about this then maybe this is in fact fundamentally wrong.

MacFarlane's incoherent political commentary seems to assert that for eight years, President George W. Bush was responsible for people believing in Jesus Christ, and that having grown disillusioned with his policies, people are now making the connection between those policies and a fundamental flaw in his Christian beliefs. Someone might remind MacFarlane that Christianity has been around for more than the eight years leading up to the 2008 election.

In the same conversation, Maher asked MacFarlane if a recently perceived softening on atheism in the media is a hopeful sign—to which MacFarlane replied, "I think there's a long way to go…it's overly optimistic to think it's gaining popularity with any kind of speed." (Since clips of *Family Guy* and *American Dad* appear on an atheist movie blog as positive depictions of atheism, he's obviously helping to move things along.)

MacFarlane's attitude is not that of someone who merely does not believe in God. He doesn't think God is a harmless fantasy like the Loch Ness monster. He's enthusiastically committed to atheism as a *superior belief system* whose time has come. And the anti-religious humor in his shows has to be viewed in the context of his personal mission to spread his superior atheist belief system.

MacFarlane isn't just any successful TV writer. His $100 million contract with FOX makes him the highest paid writer in television, and his franchise represents a $2 billion enterprise. (Just another very rich Leftist enjoying the fruits of our free market economy, but again, I digress.) MacFarlane's creative efforts constitute ninety minutes per week of primetime content. Not since Norman Lear's string of popular sitcoms in the '70s has one producer monopolized so much airtime on American television.

Here are a few examples of MacFarlane's brand of religious satire, from episodes of his shows from the 2005-2006 season:

- Jesus Christ is depicted as a teenager arguing with St. Joseph: "Up yours, Joseph! You're not my real dad!" Jesus phones Heaven, where God the Father answers while lying in bed with a woman. God hangs up on Jesus and leers at the woman, who holds up a condom. God responds: "Oh, come on, baby. It's my birthday." (FOX, *Family Guy*, November 20, 2005)

- God is shown passing gas and lighting the gas on fire. Peter explains that this is how God created the universe. (FOX, *Family Guy*, May 14, 2006)

- Alyssa invites Christ to join her at a Young Republicans meeting: "We perpetuate the ideal that Jesus chose America to destroy non-believers and brown people." (FOX, *Family Guy*, April 30, 2006)

- God descends from Heaven in the form of a shapely woman. Steve asks to see God's "boobs." God shows Steve Her breasts. (FOX, *American Dad*, November 13, 2005)

- Peter and Lois reprise the folk group they had formed years earlier called Handful of Peter (censors apparently nixed the original title, Mouthful of Peter). After smoking pot in the greenroom to calm their nerves, the couple takes to the stage and sings these lyrics:

> In God's eyes everybody's hot
> This world has beauty all through her
> Picture the fattest chick you know
> God would totally do her
> He'd do her all the way
> Even call her the next day
> To see how work was goin'.
> (FOX, *Family Guy*, April 9, 2006)

MacFarlane's contempt for the very idea of God is indicative in the shocking and vulgar situations in which he depicts God. Unlike the animated satires *The Simpsons* and *South Park* (crude as they are), MacFarlane's shows direct disdain not only at the concept of organized religion (man-made and thus obviously flawed), but often as not, at God himself. The message for viewers, then, isn't just that believers and their religions are a joke, but that the very notion of a deity is laughable at best.

...But Those Shows Aren't for Children!

MacFarlane and his apologists argue that the presence of such anti-religious (and vulgar and profane and offensive) content on television is permissible because "it's not intended for children."

It's disingenuous to argue that animated shows like *The Cleveland Show*, *Family Guy*, and *American Dad* are not meant for viewers under age fourteen. Airing on the FOX Network's "Animation Domination" block on Sunday evenings, they are preceded by the popular and relatively family-friendly *Simpsons*, and they continue through the so-called "family hour." As well, since over 70 percent of children have televisions in their bedrooms, access to content is assumed. The fact that children know the lexicon, characters, and story lines of such shows is indicative of their reach, if not their impact.

In truth, FOX works hard to promote these shows as family fare, for example running promos during NFL games with episode teasers that imply they are harmless fun. Nielsen ratings for the 2007-2008 season ranked *Family Guy* fourth overall among twelve- to seventeen-year olds, and eighth overall among two- to seven-year olds, which means hundreds of thousands of young children under age fourteen are avid fans of the show.

MacFarlane admits the idea is to lure in families on the premise that kids won't understand much of the offensive content. In a May 2010 interview with Larry King on CNN's *Larry King Live*, referring to the show *Family Guy*, King asked,

> KING: My 11 and nine year old, they love this show. They don't get it all the time. That's your purpose, right?

> MACFARLANE: That's deliberate. If we are doing our jobs right, it is the kind of thing where the parents can watch the show and get a laugh knowing exactly what we're talking about and it just goes over the kids' heads.

> KING: And you don't let them watch the DVDs.

> MACFARLANE: I wouldn't. I wouldn't, no.

And here I was thinking MacFarlane was the anti-family guy. Apparently, even MacFarlane may understand the damaging impact of watching his material on DVD, a format that permits uncensored "director's cut" versions of each TV episode, laced with even more explicit, graphic, and offensive material.

The DVDs raise an important issue, though, and one that renders moot the "adult themed" argument. In today's multi-platform media world, the idea that some content can be restricted to mature audiences is naïve at best and more likely disingenuous.

Television is just one venue to watch TV shows, and younger audiences are adept at availing themselves of other technology. The networks' web sites are virtual TV stations where full episodes are available without restriction. If kids miss an (offensive) episode of *South Park* or *Family Guy*, never fear—they can watch it online on

Hulu.com or download it to their iPods and enjoy it on the school bus. For free.

Organized Religion Is Evil

In addition to being the butt of jokes in comedy shows, religion is portrayed in American media as an "evil empire." Religious leaders and lay believers often are the antagonists, playing the part of the bad guys in shows such as *Law and Order* and *CSI*. Taking plot lines from current headlines, dramas typically depict "the church" as oppressive, outdated, and judgmental. Religious leaders (especially Catholic priests) are hypocrites who abuse their positions for power, money, or sinful pursuits.

The Parents Television Council (PTC) verified this trend in its 2006 report *Religion in a Box*. Analyzing the manner in which faith and religion were portrayed on primetime network TV, the study found, "Program format was a heavy determinant of the portrayal which religion received. Of all negative treatments of religion, 95.5% occurred on scripted drama and comedy programs. Only 4.5% of such negative treatments occurred on reality programs. Furthermore, 57.8% of positive treatments of religion also occurred on reality programs, while only 42.2% of positive portrayals occurred on scripted programs. Hollywood's disdain for religion contrasts markedly with everyday Americans who express their faith in the context of reality shows."

Perhaps the most glaring example of the formulaic vilification of organized religion is the twenty-one-year run of *Law and Order* and its offspring, *Law and Order: SVU* and *Law and Order: Criminal Intent*. The franchise prides itself for "ripping plotlines from the day's headlines," but when it comes to those that involve persons of faith, the show's writers clearly look specifically for stories that demonize clergy and believers. Since this is now the longest running show on television, I won't attempt a catalog of religious evil-doers, but a few examples reveal the franchise's favorite bigoted theme:

- *Law and Order: Criminal Intent*, "Family Values," 2009: A fundamentalist Christian husband and father goes on a murderous rampage in the name of God.
- *Law and Order: SVU*, "Sin," 2007: A gay male prostitute is murdered and the investigation reveals that a pastor who preaches extreme intolerance toward homosexuals may have had a relationship with him.
- *Law and Order*, "The Collar," 2002: A priest is killed while in a confessional and it is learned a different priest was the true target. He learns the identity of the real killer but won't betray the seal of the confessional to reveal it.
- *Law and Order: Criminal Intent*, "The Faithful," 2001: A murder that takes place in a church causes the detectives to uncover a web of deceit that reveals the illegal and immoral life of the parish priest, whose embezzlement of church funds goes to support the illegitimate (violent) son of his long-time illicit affair.

Other episodes have depicted a Christian girl who is stoned to death by her fundamentalist brother for dating a Muslim (huh?), and Orthodox Jews who are the frequent perpetrators in race-based crimes against Blacks and Hispanics.

A generation of *Law and Order* has created one of the largest syndication libraries on television. There is virtually no hour of the day in which you might not find an episode on the air, which means the legacy of this show's Leftist bias will live on for today's youth.

Lighter dramas also skewer religious believers. The FOX hit *Glee*, about a high school choral club, includes the character Quinn Fabray, the show's only outspoken Christian. Quinn, a cheerleader and the school's most popular "mean girl" also serves as president of the school's celibacy club, so naturally, she gets pregnant. The baby-daddy turns out not to be her boyfriend, Finn Hudson, but his Jewish best friend Noah "Puck" Puckerman. When Quinn's parents learn of her predicament, they react not with forgiveness and compassion, as should be expected of Christians, but with judgment and scorn, throwing her out of the house. In the season finale, Quinn's mother reappears just in time to beg her daughter's forgiveness and attend the birth of the baby, and to reveal that she has left Quinn's father, the harsh and hypocritical religious stalwart.

In its 2011 season, *Glee* dealt with the "coming out" of the character Kurt as an atheist. (He'd already come out as gay and received his first on-air kiss, from a homophobic football player, of course.) The atheism episode, entitled "Grilled Cheesus," includes Kurt's moralizing, "Sorry, but if I wanted to pay tribute to Jesus I would go to church. And the reason I don't go to church is because most churches don't think very much of gay people...or women...or science."

The same themes are found at the movie theater, where outspoken atheists like Ricky Gervais offer anti-religious bigotry disguised as teen-friendly rom-coms. With 2009's *The Invention of Lying*, the brash British comedian released a film that the United States Conference of Catholic Bishops (USCCB) Office of Film and Broadcasting called "venomous supposed comedy." The review explained,

> The fashionable "new atheism"—popularized in book form by such authors as Richard Dawkins and Christopher Hitchens—unexpectedly slithers its way into the

neighborhood Cineplex with the arrival of "The Invention of Lying."…

Set in a world where lying is unknown and every word spoken is accepted as truth, and where God does not exist until a failed documentary screenwriter (Ricky Gervais) discovers the ability to deceive and, to comfort his dying mother (Fionnula Flanagan), invents the fable of an afterlife, going on to fabricate the story of a "man in the sky" who rewards good deeds and punishes evil, all of which is eagerly accepted by the credulous masses who flock to hear his message. Along with his co-writer and co-director Matthew Robinson, Gervais launches an all-out, sneering assault on the foundations of religious faith such as has seldom if ever been seen in a mainstream film, despicably belittling core Judeo-Christian beliefs and mocking both the person and the teaching of Jesus Christ. Pervasive blasphemy, some sexual humor and references, and a few rough and crude terms.

Gervais's snide disdain for religion ranks with Seth MacFarlane's brand of anti-theism, meant not to "coexist" with people of faith (to reference the bumper sticker), but rather to tear at the very fabric of Judeo-Christian society. Oddly, Christian entertainment bloggers noted that the film didn't cause much of a ruckus along the lines of 2008's *The Golden Compass*, the family fantasy film based on the anti-Catholic books by atheist/activist Philip Pullman. It was speculated that the reason *Lying* didn't generate controversy was that Warner Bros., the distributor, buried the atheist plotline in its advertising and instead promoted the movie as a romantic comedy. On his blog, Gervais said as much, calling it a "sweet Hollywood family rom-com; it just happens to be the first ever completely atheistic movie with no concessions."

Just how important is a guy like Gervais? His hugely popular show *The Office* was exported to American TV, he's a pal and frequent guest of Jon Stewart on *The Daily Show*, and he has hosted the Golden Globe Award ceremonies. In short, he's a mainstream entertainer. Kids know him and like him.

In addition to TV and movies, young people get large doses of religious imagery through music videos. Many combine traditional religious symbolism with soft-core porn, creating confusing metaphorical messages that undermine traditional religious morality.

Performer Lady Gaga currently dominates this art form. A Madonna wannabe for a new generation, Lady Gaga (real name Stefani Joanne Angelina Germanotta) was educated in Catholic schools but has since left the Church. Her 2010 hit "Alejandro" offered an eight-minute music video that was so laden with graphic sex and blasphemous Christian and Catholic images even MTV.com asked, "Does Lady Gaga's 'Alejandro' video go too far?"

In the production, which airs on MTV and online without filters or access restrictions of any kind, Lady Gaga wears a shiny red nun's habit, provocatively swallows a rosary, simulates sex with a dozen or so nearly naked men, and ends the video with militaristic marching and what looks like a rape scene. I vote yes, MTV.

Celebrity Religion

Actress Anne Hathaway, who rose to stardom in hit children's movies such as *The Princess Diaries* and *Ella Enchanted*, made headlines in 2009 by announcing that she and her family had left the Catholic Church when her brother revealed he is gay. Explaining that she didn't click with Episcopalianism either, Hathaway was quoted, "So I'm…nothing. F—it, I'm forming. I'm a work in progress."

Hathaway is entitled to her personal religious and spiritual journey, but unfortunately, her flippant comment sums up the sentiment in Hollywood on the question of faith.

It's worth noting that the website celebatheists.com—"an offbeat collection of notables who have been public about their lack of belief in deities"—lists more than four hundred atheists, seventy-five agnostics, and a hundred or so "ambiguous" celebrities ("apparently skeptical of theism or religion"). Among those are A-list actors including George Clooney, Brad Pitt, Angelina Jolie, Morgan Freeman (who played the role of God in both *Evan Almighty* and *Bruce Almighty*), Zac Efron (of *High School Musical* fame), producer/director James Cameron (creator of *Avatar*, among others), Bruce Willis, and comedienne Kathy Griffin. It sometimes seems the only belief system that attracts celebrities is Scientology.

What does it matter whether an actor such as Zac Efron—a tween heartthrob—is a person of faith? Why should we care if a talented director like James Cameron is an atheist, as long as his movies are interesting and entertaining?

It matters because, as we well know, children absorb the influences that permeate the popular culture. The lack of belief that marks Hollywood's elite informs their creative choices and exudes from their work, and it's coming through loud and clear to America's youth.

Who Needs God Anyway?

Beyond the relentless anti-religious messages in pop culture, radical atheists have become downright aggressive about discouraging religious belief through paid media. Billboards across the nation reassure the Godless, "Don't believe in God? Join the club," and "Are you good without God? Millions are." And just in time for the Christmas season, bus riders in several large American cities now see placards featuring an affable young black man dressed in a Santa suit making a quizzical face. The message: "Why believe in a god? Just be good for goodness' sake."

I'm not arguing against humanists' right to free speech, but using a guy in a Santa suit on bus placards is the atheist advertising equivalent of "Joe Camel," attracting inner city children with a simplistic message and a familiar image. It's meant to undermine their belief in God with a child-friendly slogan, all wrapped up in a seasonal red bow.

Ho, ho, ho kids. Santa and God are both imaginary. Get the message?

Our kids do, and it's going to be our downfall if we don't work harder to combat the anti-theist march to serfdom.

PART TWO:

HOW THE LEFT INSTILL THEIR KOOL-AID VALUES

CHAPTER 4

QUEER IS THE NEW NORMAL

I n no area has the radical Left made greater inroads into the values and beliefs of America's youth than in gaining widespread acceptance of homosexuality. Should the trend of the past twenty years continue into the next generation, our grandchildren absolutely will accept homosexuality as a natural and normal form of sexual expression without any moral or even religious reservations. This total transformation in morality is now nearly inevitable. And so is the impact it will have on the cultural and social foundations upon which American civil society has stood for more than two hundred years.

How do we know the Left is succeeding in molding the attitudes and outlook of our children? Just ask the Girl Scouts.

In a 2009 study called "Good Intentions: The Beliefs and Values of Teens and Tweens Today," the Girl Scout Research Institute, in conjunction with the research firm Harris Interactive, measured the responses of more than three thousand young people on a host of issues. The longitudinal study had previously been conducted in 1989, so the questions were replicated as closely as possible in order to obtain comparative data.

On no other issue was there a greater difference between 1989 and 2009 than on the subject of homosexuality. In 1989, 31 percent of young respondents said they agreed with the statement "gay and lesbian relationships are okay, if that is a person's choice." In 2009, 59 percent agreed with that statement. (Girls were more likely to agree than boys, 65 percent to 54 percent.)

The study's conclusion? "This survey and the similar survey of 1989 show how quickly opinions on some deeply-held values can change. Whether the changes are good or bad depends on *your* values and opinions." Ah, moral relativism, thy name is Girl Scouts.

On other moral questions, the Girl Scout survey actually reveals some disenchantment with Leftist permissiveness. Fewer teens think sex before marriage is "OK if a couple loves each other" (53 percent in 1989 compared with 44 percent in 2009), and acceptance of abortion "if having a baby will change your life plans in a way that will make it hard to live" dropped slightly, from 33 percent in 1989 to 25 percent in the latest survey. (Those numbers don't necessarily translate to behavioral outcomes, but at least some moral foundations remain intact.)

Societal expectations about sexual expression, including the laws that regulate such expression, have always reflected our Judeo-Christian roots. Based on the notion that sexual intimacy is first and foremost a right of a man and a woman in the context of marriage, our cultural definition of "couplehood" served to uphold the most stable of all societal foundations: the family.

The sexual revolution of the sixties and seventies changed the definition of "couple," expanding it to include unmarried and even gay partners. Despite the moral teachings of our religious heritage, it is now considered bigoted to believe that sexual intimacy is not an entitlement for everyone. A couple is any two people who love each other in the present moment. Couples, whether heterosexual or homosexual, come and go. The purpose of coupling isn't to create stability for the individuals or the community, but to satisfy the urges and desires of those in the relationship.

Moreover, the latest number in the Left's repertoire is the good news that it's actually beneficial for kids to grow up in "sexually progressive" environments. For example, an article at LiveScience.com claims, "Children raised by lesbians do just fine, studies show." According to the latest findings, it's important to have two parents but it doesn't matter if they are two women or a woman and a man. The kids achieve about the same academic success, experience about the same level of delinquency, and report about the same levels of well-being. So I guess that's fine, then.

In an April 2011 *Time* magazine story, a headline reassured readers, "Gay-friendly communities are good for straight kids, too." In this story we learn that communities with more openly gay couples, more registered Democrats, and more Gay Straight Alliance (GSA) chapters in the schools are the places where fewer teens commit suicide. In fact gay, lesbian, and bi-sexual teens are 20 percent more likely to attempt suicide in "socially and politically conservative" areas. More proof conservatives are evil, right?

Ok, so what next? If in the span of only about fifty years we've redefined the purpose of coupling and the acceptability of formerly taboo expressions of sexuality, and we've established that there's "no bad outcome" to children as a result of such non-traditional coupling, and even that kids "do better" in such sexually progressive environments, the logical destination is...*sexual fluidity.*

Sounds gross. And it is, but not in the way you're thinking.

The radical Left now offers up a Kool-Aid to quench the thirst of every sexually vulnerable young person (that would be all of them). It goes like this: just because you're born with certain body parts doesn't mean you have to define your gender that way. You get to pick.

Sounds nuts, right? Imagine sitting down with your thirteen-year-old son for "the talk" and including this outrageous piece of information: "Charlie, don't feel constrained by your physical appearance. Your sexuality may be expressed in many ways at different times in your life. Stay open. Be available. It's all cool."

Not a conversation you're likely to have any time soon. No worries, there are folks at Charlie's school who are happy to indoctrinate him in the radical notion that human sexuality and gender identity aren't God-given but are relics of an uptight, hyper-religious, patriarchal society.

Before our children are old enough to shop for mom jeans and minivans, mark my words: America will be a place where all children are required to learn (and thus believe) that gender confusion isn't a disorder but a normal phase of human development, and that differences between men and women are irrelevant, destructive, and useless.

Think I'm over-reacting? Perhaps. But then again, maybe you haven't been paying close attention.

An Eye-popping Pop Quiz

Here's a classic example of how the Left is getting its radical ideas about "sexual fluidity" into the minds of our children. In October

2010, seventh graders at Washington, D.C.'s Hardy Middle School were administered a "sex test."

The first question for the eleven- and twelve-year olds was "What is your gender?" They could choose from four answers: "Male, female, transgender (male to female), or transgender (female to male)." Subsequent questions on the survey were, if possible, even more distressing:

How sure are you that you . . .
   . . . Can name all four body fluids that can transmit HIV?
   . . . Know the difference between oral, vaginal, and anal sex?
   . . . Can correctly put a condom on yourself or your partner?
   . . . Will avoid getting yourself or your partner pregnant if you have sex?
   . . . Can convince a reluctant partner to use barrier protection (i.e. condoms, dental dams) during sex?

Confused by terms with which they were unfamiliar, some students had no choice but to ask the survey administrator to define certain words and phrases, much to their embarrassment.

Other questions on the survey asked about the seventh graders' sexual habits and drug use:

In the past 30 days on how many days did you . . .
   . . . Have 5 or more drinks of alcohol in a row, or within a couple of hours?
   . . . Use marijuana?

... Use other non-injecting drugs (like cocaine, PCP, ecstasy)?

... Inject drugs with a needle (like heroin)?

... Have sex?

... Have sex after drinking alcohol or getting high?

You may wonder, what seventh grader would answer such questions? You'd have to figure that a middle schooler engaged in such activities knows better than to admit it.

Not to worry, the opening paragraph of the survey reassured students that their answers would remain strictly confidential: "This questionnaire asks you about sex and drugs (like cigarettes, alcohol, ecstasy and marijuana.) Please answer each question honestly, based on what you really do, think, and feel. Your answers will not be told to anyone in your school or family."

The Hardy Middle School "sex test" actually was a research and assessment tool used in conjunction with a program called "Making Proud Choices!" Offered by D.C. Public Schools (DCPS) in partnership with Metro TeenAIDS and City Year Washington, DC, the program supposedly was—according to literature from Metro TeenAIDS—"selected by DCPS for instruction to meet [health learning standards] for the middle school grades and is used in 7th and 8th health classes [sic] throughout DCPS." As a matter of fact, the material in the assessment survey itself diverged quite a bit from the board of education's abstinence-based guidelines for appropriate sex and health information for seventh graders.

But never mind that. Metro TeenAIDS is on a mission, and they're well funded, with nearly $100,000 in contracts from DCPS and a $750,000 grant from the Substance Abuse and Mental Health Services Administration of the U.S. Department of Health and

Human Services (HHS). Clearly, they have a mandate to corrupt the childhood innocence of thousands of metro DC youth.

There was another problem with the "sex test" at Hardy Middle School. Parents of the eleven- and twelve-year olds who were surveyed were not informed in advance that their children would be subject to the graphic and embarrassing questions on the assessment—much less that their children would be part of a research and educational program conducted by Metro TeenAIDS. Oddly enough, a letter to parents explaining the program and offering them the opportunity to "opt out" on behalf of their children was sent home on the very day the "sex test" was administered, too late for parents to prevent the children from participating.

A mistake? Or perhaps an intentional effort to keep parents in the dark while their children were exploited for the sake of Leftist activism. Hardy Middle School parents were understandably shocked to learn from their mortified and distraught children about the "sex test" and the school's plans to teach seventh graders about highly sensitive and inappropriate topics. Their indignation prompted the principal to "put on hold" plans to implement the Metro TeenAIDS educational program beyond the pre-test that measured students' awareness of topics kids their age shouldn't know about in the first place. (As for the confidentiality of responses, though students were told their answers couldn't be connected to their identities, parents who demanded that their children's surveys be returned were, in fact, able to retrieve their children's answers.)

Unfortunately, programs such as this one—and the surreptitious indoctrination of our children with radical sex and sexuality training—no longer are surprising or uncommon. Nor are they being conducted only under the radar.

Thanks to radicals from the NEA and elsewhere, explicit sex education programs are being mandated by state legislatures across the nation. They're coming soon to an elementary school near you, and they open the door to teach the radical Left's redefined notions of sexuality and gender identity.

Too Sexy for Your Childhood

In February 2011, Diane Schneider, a health teacher from Ramapo High School in Spring Valley, New York, represented the LGBT Caucus of the National Education Association (NEA) as part of the UN Commission on the Status of Women's 55th Session, at a presentation entitled, "Sexuality, Homophobia and Transphobia: The Need to Improve Access to Education and Work."

There, on behalf of the educational establishment of the United States of America, and tacitly of our government, Schneider said, "Homophobia exists when those stuck in the binary box of 'strictly hetero' find themselves slipping out of that role that religion and family promote."

Schneider explained,

> The question comes to mind how we as educators can serve to eradicate homo- and trans-phobia through education.... The key to the answer lies in the realization that both gender identity expression, as well as sexual orientation, [is] a spectrum and not a box that houses our being.... *We must teach our children at a very young age that being male, female or inter-sexed comes with the presence of genitalia and no further expectations.* [emphasis added]

Let me translate, just in case the significance of Schneider's statement is lost in her linguistic gobbledygook. Because of backward notions taught by their parents and in their churches, American children are homophobes. Educators can eliminate homophobia by undermining the lessons about human sexuality taught at home and in church, and indoctrinating children from a very young age to believe instead that gender and sexual orientation are *social and cultural constructs*. You're born with body parts, but they don't mean anything. You get to choose your gender and your sexual orientation. In fact, you may not be one thing or another, but rather express your sexuality along a continuum of attractions and interests.

That's not all. Ms. Schneider also said that to help children grow to "be their authentic self, free of society's gender expectations," they should receive "comprehensive" sexuality education—not sex ed as presented in a human biology class—but specifically an approach that includes "terms such as orgasm, oral sex and masturbation." This is crucial, she says, because we ought not to teach our children that sex is primarily associated with reproduction, as that would "provide the subtle message to LGBT youth that their intimacy does not count."

Diane Schneider also is co-chair of her local chapter of GLSEN, the Gay, Lesbian, Straight Education Network. But most importantly, she's a teacher and the advisor to the Gay Straight Alliance (GSA) in her school. In other words, she's part of the national network of radical gay activists with a daily influence over children, as well as over the development and implementation of curricula in America's public schools.

But teachers and activists like Diane Schneider are only the foot soldiers in the battle against traditional values about sexuality and gender identity. The general who has led the charge against traditional, religious, and family values about sex is Kevin Jennings, President Obama's notorious former director of the Office of Safe and Drug Free Schools in the U.S. Department of Education.

As one of Obama's infamous czars, Jennings was supposed to be working to make schools safer for all children. As it turns out, he mostly used his job to promote the gay political agenda. Jennings is the founder of GLSEN, which he created as a high school teacher in Massachusetts. That was around the time when, according to his autobiography, he counseled a minor student to practice "safe sex" and use a condom after the student confided in Jennings that he had had a homosexual liaison with an adult man.

Never mind that teachers are required by law to report such confidences to Child Protective Services because sex between adults and children is criminal child abuse. Jennings supported the boy's right to explore his sexuality. Ironic career twist: Kevin Jennings was the *Safe* Schools Czar.

GLSEN seeks to dismantle "institutional heterosexism"—that is, the "myth" of "heteronormativity," the belief that heterosexuality is typically normal. (It's not?) Highlighting the role of schools in this effort, a 2002 GLSEN report said,

> … despite those who would like education to focus solely on scholastic aptitude, schools have always been places where societal values are transmitted and prejudices of all kinds routinely addressed. Where heterosexism causes uneven social and learning opportunities—and it does everywhere—it stands to reason that schools would want to squarely face the issue and level this imbalance.

Thanks to a drumbeat of indoctrination, the core beliefs about sexuality promoted by GLSEN are overtaking health curricula from

Maine to California and everywhere in between. And despite parental and community objections, the movement to expand radical
sexuality education is building steam.

Case in point: the proposed sexuality education curriculum in
Helena, Montana included these educational goals and benchmarks:

- Kindergarten and first grade: "understand that human
  beings can love people of the same gender and people
  of another gender."
- Second grade: understand that "making fun of people
  by calling them gay (e.g. 'homo,' 'fag,' 'queer') is disre-
  spectful and hurtful."
- Third and fourth grade: understand that the media
  often presents unrealistic images of sex, marriage, and
  parenthood. (Fair enough, but who defines "realistic"?)
- Fifth grade: understand the safety hazards of hooking
  up online, and a brief definition of abstinence (which
  is never repeated again in the curriculum at any grade
  level).
- Sixth grade: learn that "sexual intercourse includes
  but is not limited to vaginal, oral, or anal penetration;
  using the penis, fingers, tongue or objects." (This lesson is repeated every year from sixth through twelfth
  grade.) Also in sixth grade, cover STDs and AIDS, and
  an introduction to the idea of gender identity (different from sexual orientation).
- Seventh and eighth grades: understand that the
  U.S. Supreme Court has ruled, "that to a certain extent,
  people have the right to make personal decisions con-
  cerning sexuality and reproductive health matters,
  such as abortion, sterilization and contraception."

(In other words, you don't have to tell your mom or dad if you want to get condoms, go on the Pill, or have an abortion.) Also, understand state laws governing the age of consent.

- High school: more about intercourse, plus information on sexual abuse, safe sex, dating violence, sexual exploitation, and sexual orientation, as well as "understanding that erotic images in art reflect a society's views about sexuality and help people understand sexuality." (Pornography is positive and culturally significant.)

Montana educators spent two years developing this material. Rather than seeking input from parents or religious leaders, they modeled this "evidence-based" curriculum on Guidelines for Comprehensive Sexuality Education (Third Edition), Kindergarten through 12th Grade, produced by the National Guidelines Task Force.

The National Guidelines Task Force was formed in 1991 by the Sexuality Information and Education Council of the United States (SIECUS). SIECUS, in turn, was founded in 1964 by Dr. Mary S. Calderone, former medical director for the Planned Parenthood Federation, along with a small group of Leftist professors. SIECUS spearheads the National Coalition to Support Sexuality Education, a virtual "Who's Who" of Leftist groups from the ACLU to the Sierra Club. And, for the past fifty years it has been at the forefront of the movement to infiltrate schools with so-called "comprehensive" sexuality education—note the use of the word "sexuality" and not "sex." Beyond basic biology, these folks want to teach Leftist values about sex, gender, and relationships.

Thankfully, parents in Helena were paying attention. When the completed final draft of the curriculum made its way to the school board, members of the community were there to object. Of course, they were portrayed in the media as backward, homophobic, religious fundamentalists. But whatever. They won.

Or at least, the published curriculum that was officially adopted by the Helena School Board was heavily edited to take out the most controversial language. But remember the Hardy Middle School "sex test"? School board guidelines are no guarantee that something much more explicit—and much more Leftist—about sex won't actually be taught in school.

Meanwhile countless other school districts have incorporated the philosophy of "comprehensive" sexuality education into their health classes, so parents must remove their children from class to protect their innocence and uphold their sexual values.

But that assumes you know about the lessons in advance. In the spring of 2010, parents in Shenandoah, Iowa, learned after the fact that their eighth graders had been subject to a Planned Parenthood sexual education class that demonstrated, among other things, how to perform an exam of female genitalia, how to put on a condom, and how to assume specific sexual positions (stuffed animals were used to teach this lesson; don't ask). Parents also objected that photographs used in the class were pornographic. "As far as we were concerned, it wasn't sex ed, it was sex demonstration," one parent said.

Bullying Is Bad, Unless It Helps Progressives

In any case, opting out of sex education classes won't work for long because issues of sexuality now are presented under the aegis of "school safety."

Here's the rationale: being gay means being bullied, and bullying is a safety issue, not a health issue. Ergo, children can be required to undergo mandatory "school safety" training. And parents may not opt out.

That's how the curriculum was framed in the Alameda (California) Unified School District (AUSD), where, in 2009-2010, parents filed lawsuits and threatened a recall election to keep their kindergarten through third grade children from a mandatory lesson on homosexual relationships as part of a nine-lesson anti-bullying curriculum.

The controversy over "Lesson 9," in which children would be taught specific concepts and language about homosexuality and gender identity, led the AUSD to abandon that portion of its program—but only because the lesson focused exclusively on bullying as an expression of homophobia, and didn't specifically mention any other "protected classes" besides gays, such as racial minorities or people with physical disabilities. It simply wasn't PC enough. The lesson was reinstituted once this glitch was ironed out.

Funnily enough, it turns out that bullying gay kids is not even an issue in the elementary schools of AUSD. Documentation from the District obtained by the Pacific Justice Institute (PJI) revealed "that, of the approximately one-hundred-seventy incident reports in an eighteen month period, there were no school incidents of harassment due to sexual orientation in the elementary grades. The vast majority of reported complaints on AUSD campuses involved opposite-sex sexual harassment and racial tension, not sexual orientation."

No matter. An agenda is an agenda. AUSD's literature-based program includes books for first graders such as *Who's in a Family?* by Robert Skutch ("…Robin's family is made up of her dad, Clifford, her dad's partner, Henry, and Robin's cat, Sassy").

In second grade, students read, *And Tango Makes Three* by Justin Richardson and Peter Parnell. Surely you've read it. It's the story of two male penguins, Roy and Silo, described as being "a little bit different": "They didn't spend much time with the girl penguins, and the girl penguins didn't spend much time with them," it says. When these male penguins hatch an egg, they decide, "We'll call her Tango because it takes two to make a Tango." The book claims, "Tango was the very first penguin in the zoo to have two daddies."

To teach third graders about the variety of family structures, students watch a film called *That's a Family,* featuring some homosexual couples as well as traditional families. The curriculum also includes a list of LGBT vocabulary words that students must learn.

It's no wonder parents fought this curriculum. But, the reality is, fights against school districts like AUSD or Helena or Shenandoah are minor battles. Leftists know that the key to implementing wholesale sexual indoctrination of children in the American public school system is to mandate anti-discrimination measures at the federal level, which will be accomplished relatively easily by marching under the anti-bullying banner. That's why during his tenure at the Department of Education, Jennings marshaled the Leftists in Congress to propose broad legislation that will give him unmitigated power to implement "comprehensive" sexuality education under the guise of "school safety" and "anti-bullying."

After all, no one is for bullying. Who could vote against a law to protect kids from bullying and live to tell about it back home in the district?

But a careful reading of the proposed legislation introduced in the 111th Congress and still floating in committees of the 112th proves that Jennings wants to legislate wholesale cultural change.

The Senate version of the Student Nondiscrimination Act of 2010, S.3390, and the House version, H.R. 4530, include some expansive and extraordinary measures that would

- Prohibit public school students from being excluded from participating in, or subject to discrimination under, any federally-assisted educational program on the basis of their actual or perceived sexual orientation or gender identity or that of their associates.
- Consider harassment to be a form of discrimination.
- Prohibit retaliation against anyone for opposing conduct they reasonably believe to be unlawful under this Act.
- Authorize federal departments and agencies to enforce these prohibitions by cutting off educational assistance to recipients found to be violating them.
- Deem a state's receipt of federal educational assistance for a program to constitute a waiver of sovereign immunity for conduct prohibited under this Act regarding such program.

In practice, this means schools won't be allowed to maintain gender-specific facilities, teams, or clubs; prevent a transgender student from using the bathroom or locker room of his/her choice; or prohibit a student from dressing in drag for school or at school functions. Or else they risk losing federal funding and subject themselves to potential lawsuits.

In other words, the message to public schools is, Normalize homosexuality and transgenderism, or else.

More Than Just Gay Rights—Sex for Kids of All Ages

The purpose of "comprehensive sexuality" is supposed to be reducing teenage pregnancies and the rate of sexually transmitted diseases among young people. Just as the "school safety" angle justifies the gay agenda in schools, the Left cites a public health imperative to allow them to expose children and teens to graphic materials and instruction about sex.

Of course, the first thing Leftists do is dismiss the efficacy of abstinence-only sex ed on the grounds that it "doesn't work." (Or maybe because it promotes abstinence. Where's the fun in that?)

Instead, although the human species has somehow, pretty much since the dawn of time, managed to figure out how intercourse works, Leftist educators like those in Helena believe the mechanics should be taught—not just once, but every year from grades six through twelve.

The reasoning behind this unnecessarily over-explicit level of education in the classroom has been articulated clearly by the International Planned Parenthood Federation (IPPF) in a 2010 report called "Stand and Deliver: Sex, health and young people in the 21st century."

IPPF is the international umbrella for 180 Planned Parenthood organizations worldwide. Its political agenda includes population control through contraception and abortion, as well as the broad promotion of "sexual rights." It works closely with the UN and other international groups to promote social and political change in support of its Leftist views of sexuality.

Those views are summed up in seven principles of "sexual rights," among them, "Sexuality is an integral part of the personhood of every human being, for this reason a favorable environment in which everyone may enjoy all sexual rights as part of the process of development must be created" and "Sexuality, and pleasure deriving from it, is a central aspect of being human."

IPPF's report on sexuality in young people—loosely defined, but including anyone over the age of ten—expands on these rights to include children. "The evolving capacities of the child include his or her physiological ability to reproduce, his or her psychological ability to make informed decisions about counseling and health care, and his or her emotional and social ability to engage in sexual behaviors in accordance with the responsibilities and roles that this entails."

Among the recommendations IPPF makes to governments around the globe is mandatory sexual education for children age ten and older to include "the pleasures of sex." Apparently, despite being "sexual beings," kids won't know sex is pleasurable unless you tell them.

The report specifically calls out organized religions, including the Catholic Church and Islam, for promoting sexual repression: "Young people's sexuality is still contentious for many religious institutions…. Currently, many religious teachings deny the pleasurable and positive aspects of sex, and limited guidelines for sexual education often focus on abstinence before marriage."

IPPF, clearly believing sexual freedom for young people outweighs any wisdom that might possibly be enshrined in thousands of years of religious doctrine, offers this nugget of advice:

> Each religion or faith must find a way of explaining and providing guidance on issues of sex and sexual relationships among young people, *which supports rather than denies their experiences and needs.* By highlighting strong values in faiths and religions, and *overcoming stigma and stereotypes that religious conventions perpetuate*, communities and leaders can help improve young people's access to sexual and reproductive health information and services, and so improve their health and well-being. [emphasis added]

If you can get through the jargon, you understand that IPPF advocates that government leaders usurp the rights of parents to instill their religious beliefs and values about sexual morality in their children—so as to improve "access to sexual and reproductive health information and services" for all young people.

Coincidentally, those services are largely provided by Planned Parenthood.

"Stand and Deliver" is secular-progressive, free-love propaganda, and anti-religious bigotry disguised as a public health white paper. Isn't that exactly what we need from our government and the hordes of activists working night and day "for our children"? I don't know about you, but that's not my idea of "safe schools."

CHAPTER 5

READIN', WRITIN', REVOLUTION

O ur kids are not as well educated as their peers around the world. In fact, they're no better educated than American students of two generations ago—despite massive real-dollar increases in education spending.

The reality is that American kids have fallen way behind the international competition. According to the 2010 assessment administered by the Organization for Economic Cooperation and Development, the U.S. ranked twenty-third or twenty-fourth out of sixty-five countries in most subjects on the Program for International Student Assessment (PISA). A gold star for the children of Shanghai who made the Chinese people proud by acing the test in their first year of participation!

And according to 2011 congressional testimony by Andrew Coulson, director of the Center for Educational Freedom at the Cato

Institute, American schools are not improving: "We spent over $151,000 per student sending the class of 2009 through public schools. That is nearly three times as much as we spent on the graduating class of 1970, adjusting for inflation. Despite that massive real spending increase, overall achievement has stagnated or declined, depending on the subject."

The truth about American public schools: they're just not getting it done. A Gallup poll shows roughly 80 percent of American adults think their own children are being well educated, but about 54 percent of us think the system as a whole is stinky. The 46 percent who are satisfied with public education in this country must be teachers.

If the radical Left is successfully toppling the three-legged stool of American culture and society by undermining our children's faith, their understanding of "family," and their commitment to freedom and free enterprise, surely these Kool-Aid vendors must be doing so for the benefit of our nation's youngest generation?

Not so much.

Not only is the Left reducing American exceptionalism to the trash-heap of traditional values. They're also busy assuring we can never be exceptional in the future. How? By under-educating our children into the most measurable decline towards mediocrity that an educational system has ever achieved.

If ever-increasing spending on education isn't improving the outcome for our students, we must infer that there is a problem that money cannot solve. And there is. It's ideology.

Studies of teacher attitudes and opinions bear this out. For example, in a survey of public and private high school history teachers commissioned by the American Enterprise Institute, teachers revealed it is more important to them that students learn to celebrate the diversity among the different ethnic, religious, and immigrant groups living in the U.S.A. than to know the common history that defines our past, including dates, names, locations, and important events.

And *37 percent* even said it is "absolutely essential" that they teach their students to become activists who will seek change in our political system, while only one in six think it is essential that students understand concepts such as federalism, the separation of powers, or checks and balances. So, will they know what to change when they get the chance to do it? (Nah, they'll just hope it changes.)

If mastery of subject matter is only a peripheral purpose of education for these educators, you have to wonder what they mean by "education." What kinds of teachers would use the power of the classroom to instill a biased, unchallenged, unquestioned political point of view in their students? What sorts of folks serve up classroom Kool-Aid like mother's milk, in an effort to manipulate and mold our young citizens to adopt a skewed, socialist worldview?

Why, the kind who are educated in America's pre-eminent schools of education and subsequently become part of the public school system, of course. Now, before you start defending the lovely young lady who teaches your son's kindergarten class, or the sharp-as-a-tack seasoned educator who got all of your kids through high school algebra, a caveat: not every teacher is a Leftist. (Maybe every teacher in Wisconsin, but that would figure, right?)

But by virtue of their mandatory training in education theory, most teachers currently working in American classrooms have been at least exposed to some of the nation's most radical proponents of progressivism. What's worse, many of them don't even realize that getting a teaching certificate essentially means being recruited into a political movement.

Who's Teaching the Teachers?

Remember Bill Ayers? That guy who happened to live in Barack Obama's trendy Hyde Park neighborhood—someone Obama saw and talked to a few times, but "not somebody who I exchange ideas from [sic] on a regular basis."

Of course, they did serve together for several years on the boards of two organizations: the philanthropic Woods Foundation and the Chicago Annenberg Challenge (CAC), the failed $49.2 million grant program intended to improve Chicago's public schools. And in 1995, Ayers hosted a coffee klatch at his home to help launch Obama's candidacy for the Illinois State house. They probably didn't "exchange ideas" then, either.

Most of us know Ayers and his wife, Bernardine Dohrn, as founders of the Weather Underground, the domestic terrorism group that conducted bombings, including of the U.S. Capitol, between 1970 and 1974 to protest the Vietnam War. Ayers calls the Weatherman actions "armed propaganda" or "acts of vandalism," not terrorism. He specializes in semantics, as you'll soon see.

What most people don't appreciate is that for the forty-odd years between his revolutionary days as a self-proclaimed and unrepentant domestic "armed propagandist" and his renown as an early supporter of Barack Obama, Bill Ayers became one of the nation's pre-eminent educators of America's teachers.

Until his retirement in August 2010, Ayers was Distinguished Professor of Education and Senior University Scholar at the University of Illinois at Chicago (UIC). He has published numerous books on teaching and is a frequent speaker at colleges of education across the country. When people refer to the "education elite"—the folks whose research, theories, and writings guide the practice of education in our nation's classrooms—Ayers is among the most revered and respected in the nation.

Not only are Leftists like Bill Ayers molding the formation of America's teaching brigade, they also are shaping the curriculum that our Leftist-trained teachers will implant. Ayers himself served as a vice president and head of the curriculum committee for the prestigious American Educational Research Association. AERA, founded in 1916 and currently boasting 25,000 member educators, is the leading international professional organization for the dissemination of research about the teaching profession.

It's crucial to understand how deeply the Left believes in the political purpose of schools. Secretary of Education Arne Duncan has said, "To get the kind of *transformational change* that we as a country need takes a huge amount of courage. The status quo isn't working for lots and lots of children in this country.... We have to get a lot better with a huge sense of urgency because the stakes are so high.... But the most courage is [shown by] those leaders who are doing the hard work every day in the classrooms and the schools" [emphasis added].

I agree that the stakes are high, but Duncan's idea of "transformational change" scares me, especially when he's talking about our children's classrooms.

Interestingly, Obama and Duncan aren't nearly radical enough for the educational elitists who actually control American education. While the Obama administration talks about school reform, competition, charter schools, and an even greater emphasis on standardized tests as measures of success, the radicals in education want less structure and more freedom to pursue "democracy" rather than knowledge. Ayers lobbied for Obama to appoint an anti-testing, anti-accountability professor from Stanford's school of education, Linda Darling-Hammond, rather than Duncan as secretary of Education. Perhaps Obama and Ayers don't spend much time "exchanging ideas" after all—since Ayers didn't get his wish on that one.

But Ayers' influence in American education is inarguably significant. For Leftists such as Ayers, American schools are the perfect venue to practice and promote collectivism. Progressives in education like to use "democracy" (small "d") when describing the goal of education, using the term in its strictly socialist sense. As Ayers says, "What makes education in a democracy distinct is a commitment to a particularly precious and fragile ideal, the belief that the fullest development of all is the necessary condition for the full development of each; conversely, the fullest development of each is necessary for the full development of all."

Sounds a lot like Obama's oft-repeated declaration that, "Our individual salvation depends on collective salvation." Both Ayers' and Obama's statements are platitudes of liberation theology and euphemisms for "redistribution of wealth."

In fact, the ultimate agenda of teacher training can be summed up in Ayers' statement to education students at National-Louis University. Tipping the hand of elite Leftists about the real purpose of American education, the former Weatherman said, "We should commit ourselves in every way we can think of to imagining education, and practicing education as the practice of enlightenment, the practice of freedom, the practice of social justice...the doing of social justice."

And we wonder why our nation's schools are failing our children. (Get it? Failing?)

Leftism in Teacher Education—the Rule, Not the Exception

It's important to acknowledge that not all of America's school-teachers are out to indoctrinate our youth into a mindless acceptance of socialism. The vast majority of rank and file teachers are caring, committed educators who do what they do because they love children and they have a heart for teaching. They mean well.

Yet by every measurable standard, our public school system as a whole is failing. Student performance on standardized tests and high school graduation rates have declined even as spending per pupil has risen. How can we pour ever-increasing resources into this school system and consistently get worse and worse results?

Suppose, though, that the folks engaged in preparing America's teachers don't think declining test scores or falling graduation rates are an indication of "the problem." Mind you, they aren't any happier with our schools than the rest of us, but they don't believe the issue is a lack of student performance or teacher competency.

The educational establishment has an entirely different set of goals and priorities from parents with respect to educating our nation's children. Examined through the prism of the Left's socialist objectives, the connection between how teachers are trained and the results we see in the pitiful education of our children makes a strange kind of sense. The radically Leftist post-secondary education machine has, for more than a half-century, churned out educators who believe their job is one thing (molding the citizens of tomorrow for "democracy" and "social justice"), when really their job ought to be something else entirely (imparting knowledge and skills for an informed and competent citizenry). If only standardized tests measured empathy, the ability to recognize capitalist and racial oppression, and one's sense of obligation to fight systemic injustice. America's students might be numero uno among industrialized nations!

Pedagogy of Pedagogy

If you're anything like me, you may be asking how in the world our education system has wandered so far from the mission of imparting knowledge to the goal of enacting social change. Since the early twentieth century, trends in teaching have been influenced by the most extreme figures on the Left. Beginning with humanist and avowed socialist John Dewey in the 1930s, the education arena has attracted outspoken Leftists who understand that their socialist ideas can be imposed on young people without resistance. Moreover, they couch their Leftist agendas in fuzzy educational jargon that disguises their radical socialist goals. This is why aspiring teachers don't even realize what they're being fed.

One of the most important of these theories is critical pedagogy, developed by Brazilian socialist educator Paulo Freire and articulated in his iconic tome, *Pedagogy of the Oppressed*, first published in1968. Freire, working among the poor and downtrodden in Brazil in the 1950s, incorporated the concepts of liberation theology into his educational philosophy. (Note: an extension of this movement is Black Liberation Theology, practiced by Obama's former pastor, the Reverend Jeremiah Wright. It's all starting to make sense, isn't it?)

Freire's book is a paean to socialism. Though it had been published only in Portuguese, it took the educational world by storm and earned Freire a visiting professorship in 1969 at Harvard University. (Act surprised.) His book was published in English the next year.

According to a 2003 survey of the nation's top schools of education, *Pedagogy of the Oppressed* is still one of the most frequently assigned books for education students. Sol Stern, an education reform expert and senior fellow of the Manhattan Institute, explained how this "pedagogy" is only about raising self-awareness of oppression, not about teaching and learning. In a Spring 2009 *City Journal* article, Stern pointed out,

The odd thing is that Freire's magnum opus isn't, in the end, about education—certainly not the education of children. *Pedagogy of the Oppressed* mentions none of the issues that troubled education reformers throughout the twentieth century: testing, standards, curriculum, the role of parents, how to organize schools, what subjects should be taught in various grades, how best to train teachers, the most effective way of teaching disadvantaged students. This ed-school bestseller is, instead, a utopian political tract calling for the overthrow of capitalist hegemony and the creation of classless societies. Teachers who adopt its pernicious ideas risk harming their students— and ironically, their most disadvantaged students will suffer the most.

Stern also reveals the true intention of Freire's critical pedagogy by noting that the footnotes in his book are not from world-famous educators such as Dewey, Piaget, or Maria Montessori, but from communists and socialists—Marx, Lenin, Mao, Che Guevara, and Fidel Castro.

We shouldn't wonder why our schools of education are so enthralled with the work of Freire. Among the education elite, the most prestigious members of this highly selective fraternity are also the most radical. For example, UCLA's Peter McLaren is considered one of America's gurus of "critical pedagogy." Known as a freakishly prolific writer and speaker, he is a frequent presenter at schools of education with talks such as "Critical Pedagogy as a Global Movement for Social Justice" and "Global Capitalism and the Crisis in Education." A visit to his website will have you humming along to revolutionary tunes about Che, whose image is also tattooed on

McLaren's arm. Look up "aging hippy" in the dictionary, and you'll find his photo.

Like McLaren, Bill Ayers makes no secret of his true motives for being involved in education. Once quoted as saying, "In a sense, all education is about power" (but not "knowledge is power"), he believes the purpose of teaching has almost nothing to do with building a student's knowledge base, but everything to do with transformation and "revolution."

In a keynote address at the 2006 World Education Forum in Caracas, Venezuela, Ayers waxed nostalgic about his early years as a teacher and reflected on the moment when he realized the potential political power of the classroom:

> I began teaching when I was 20 years old in a small free-dom school affiliated with the Civil Rights Movement in the United States. The year was 1965, and I'd been arrested in a demonstration. Jailed for ten days, I met several activists who were finding ways to link teaching and education with deep and fundamental social change.... I walked out of jail and into my first teaching position—and from that day until this I've thought of myself as a teacher, but I've also understood teaching as a project intimately connected with social justice.... As students and teachers begin to see themselves as linked to one another, as tied to history and capable of collective action, the fundamental message of teaching shifts slightly, and becomes broader, more generous: we must change ourselves as we come together to change the world. Teaching invites transformations, it urges revolu-tions small and large. La educacion es revolucion!

Now, you might say, "Well, that's Bill Ayers. Everyone knows he's a bomb-throwing radical. But there's no one like him teaching at my kid's elementary school."

Want to bet? Virtually every classroom teacher in America today is prepared in a college of education where the likes of Bill Ayers have changed the focus of these programs so that preparing teachers for subject-matter expertise is only peripherally important. Ayers even declares it an "educational myth" that teachers must be experts in their subjects! This explains a lot, doesn't it?

Instead, schools of education are all about training "change agents" who will use the classroom to correct society's ills through the widespread infusion of "social justice."

Stern outlined the wholesale takeover of Education schools in a 2006 *City Journal* piece in which he traced Ayers' "aha moment" about the political power of the classroom to his instruction by Freirian professor Maxine Greene at Columbia Teachers College:

> Greene told future teachers that they could help change this bleak landscape by developing a "transformative" vision of social justice and democracy in their classrooms. Her vision, though, was a far cry from the democratic optimism of the Founding Fathers, Abraham Lincoln, and Martin Luther King Jr., which most parents would endorse.... *The education professors feel themselves anointed to use the nation's K–12 classrooms to resist [America's] oppressive system. Thus Maxine Greene urged teachers not to mince words with children about the evils of the existing social order.... In other words, they should turn the little ones into young socialists and critical theorists.* [emphasis added]

Thus, according to Stern,

> One by one, the education schools are lining up behind
> social justice teaching and enforcing it on their students—
> especially since they expect aspiring teachers to possess
> the approved liberal "dispositions," or individual charac-
> ter traits, that will qualify them to teach in the public
> schools.

Embarrassingly, for example, at my alma mater, Michigan State
University (the school of education ranked number one in the nation
for the past sixteen years), future educators will learn to teach science for social justice, environmental literacy for socio-ecological
action and policy, a "hidden curriculum" in the mathematics classroom, and racial identity and self-concepts in the urban classroom.

The tragedy of American public education in our time is that the
radicals who claim to advocate for the liberation and educational
equality of our nation's poor and minority children are, in fact, seal-
ing their doom. Freire may have taught indigent Brazilians to read
back in 1950, but as Stern concludes, Freire's socialist theories
masquerading as a pedagogical framework constitute "educational
malpractice" sweeping America in our day. This doesn't stop the
Chicago-based Teachers for Social Justice from hosting a Freire
Forum, however, to help "build a movement of education for liberation!"

Thanks to the hogwash being foisted on teachers under the guise
of "critical pedagogy," American students are no longer getting a
rigorous, academic education—especially our poorest students, for
whom a proper education could be the key to lift them out of poverty
and assure greater equality. Instead, they're getting a dumbed-down
curriculum that teaches activism through "community based

learning," preparing them only to be sub-literate citizens and community organizers, not successful, productive citizens.

For contrast, look at the strides being made in the Harlem Children's Zone by educator Geoffrey Canada and the Promise Academy Charter Schools. In a one-hundred-block section of New York's highest-risk neighborhood, traditional education works just as well as in any tony suburb, not because teachers accommodate "injustice" with bogus theories about pedagogy and curricula designed to validate students' victim status, but because they assure that every child receives hands-on instruction to achieve measurable academic success.

Closer to Ayers' Chicago neighborhood, there are the impressive Urban Prep Academies, begun in 2006 as the nation's first charter public high schools for boys. The school motto, "We believe," is "a constant reminder that Urban Prep students will not fall into the trap of negative stereotypes and low expectations. Instead, Urban Prep students believe in their potential and believe in their ability to exceed that potential." Focusing on a rigorous academic program, required extra-curricular and community service components, and four-year preparation for college readiness, the program is already a resounding success—a full 100 percent of the school's first graduating class was accepted to at least one four-year college or university.

Yet Ayers and his education elite cohort continue to perpetuate the disastrous status quo for poor and minority children. They don't want to educate them. Instead, they want repayment of something they call the "education debt"—reparations to be paid for generations of "white supremacy" in American culture. As Ayers wrote on his website in a January 2008 essay on school reform,

> The dominant narrative in contemporary school reform
> is once again focused on exclusion and disadvantage, race

and class, black and white. "Across the US," the National Governors Association declared in 2005, "a gap in academic achievement persists between minority and disadvantaged students and their white counterparts." This is the commonly referenced and popularly understood "racial achievement gap," and it drives education policy at every level. Interestingly, whether heartfelt or self-satisfied, the narrative never mentions the monster in the room: white supremacy.

Sol Stern poses a crucial question: Why, if they're so concerned about poor and black students, do Leftist educational theorists like Ayers shortchange these children? Why do they "agitate for instruction" that holds poor kids back? Either A) They're stupid (honestly, wading through Ayers' writings does not impress), or B) They're more concerned with their own anti-American, anti-capitalist political agenda than they are with educating anybody's children, rich, poor, black, brown, or white. Or else it's C) From George Bernard Shaw's *Maxims for Revolutionists*: "Those who can't do, teach."

The correct answer is D) All of the above.

In American Education, "Look for the Union Label"

Of all the avenues the Left is using to ply the next generation with the Kool-Aid of socialism, none is more menacing or effective than its wholesale commandeering of public education through mandatory unionization of teachers. Frustrated conservatives often refer to the public education system as "government schools," but in reality our nation's children are educated in "union schools." The needs, desires, demands, and doctrine of the unions come first—no matter what they say their educational mission is.

Gosh, that's really cynical of me, huh? In fact, the notion that today's public school teachers are an overburdened, under-appreciated lot is—to use the technical term—a bunch of hooey. According to the Bureau of Labor Statistics, average teacher wages are more than the median hourly wage of accountants, architects, civil engineers, medical scientists, and other professional positions. Factor in the abbreviated work week—36.5 hours during the school year—and summers off, the incredibly generous health, life insurance, and pension benefits that come with the job, and most school districts' continuing education incentives, and you've got yourself a really good gig.

Not to mention the opportunities to increase teacher pay with added responsibilities. Become a department head, administer placement exams, coach the softball team, or direct the school play and there's your holiday bonus check. Nice work if you can get it.

For the record, my husband and I both come from long lines of educators, and we hold teachers in high esteem. We are also indebted to the teachers who have helped us to educate our four children. But even many of the teachers to whom we're close admit that America's teacher unions have created a monster. A raging, greedy, Left-wing, militant, self-serving, politicized monster—which, as we all know, is the worst kind.

Did you know that saying this makes me a "bastard"? This is the pronouncement of Bob Chanin, forty-plus-year general counsel to the NEA, speaking on the auspicious occasion of his July 2009 retirement. "Why are these conservative and right-wing bastards picking on NEA and its affiliates? I will tell you why: it is the price we pay for success. NEA and its affiliates have been singled out because they are the most effective unions in the United States. And they are the nation's leading advocates for public education and the type of liberal social and economic agenda that these groups find unacceptable...."

Chanin went on to explain the secret to the NEA's success:

> Despite what some among us would like to believe, it is not because of our creative ideas. It is not because of the merit of our positions. It is not because we care about children. And it is not because we have a vision of a great public school for every child. *NEA and its affiliates are effective advocates because we have power.* And we have power because there are more than 3.2 million people who are willing to pay us hundreds of millions of dollars in dues each year because they believe that we are the unions that can most effectively represent them, the unions that can protect their rights and advance their interests as education employees.
>
> This is not to say that the concern of NEA and its affiliates with closing achievement gaps, reducing drop-out rates, improving teacher quality, and the like are unimportant or inappropriate. To the contrary, these are the goals that guide the work we do. *But they need not and must not be achieved at the expense of due process, employee rights, and collective bargaining. That simply is too high a price to pay!*
>
> When all is said and done, NEA and its affiliates must never lose sight of the fact that they are unions, and what unions do first and foremost is represent their members. [emphasis added]

At least someone on the Left practices transparency.

Chanin's bold admission conveys the union's true priorities. And typical union-style tactics are employed to achieve these ends.

Who says teachers don't like bullying? They pay for it with their PAC contributions to the NEA.

Power such as Chanin described has its privileges. Under the current administration, one of those is access. In addition to visits with various White House staffers, Dennis Van Roekel, president of the 3.2 million-member NEA, meets with Secretary of Education Arne Duncan *once a month*. "He's very accessible," Van Roekel has said. "During the Bush administration...we didn't have any meetings with the Department of Education."

And why not meet monthly? Those three million-plus teachers can be mobilized for Democratic political campaigns with the click of a mouse. Of course, when they're called into action, the Leftist powers-that-be want to assure that they're ready to serve as "change agents" and community organizers. This explains why the NEA recommends on its web site that America's teachers read Saul Alinsky's *Rules for Radicals*.

Not even kidding.

Workers of the World, Unite—in Wisconsin!

Why exactly would American public school teachers need to learn Saul Alinsky's formula for radicals, "agitate + aggravate + educate + organize"?

For starters, to mobilize against a legitimately elected government in Wisconsin, where voters overwhelmingly chose Republican Governor Scott Walker in November 2010 on a platform of reduced spending, smaller government, and reining in the state's skyrocketing deficit.

One of the first major issues facing Governor Walker was a $137 million shortfall for the 2011 fiscal year, with an additional balance of over $225 million owed to the state's Patients' Compensation Fund, which had been raided to make up past deficits. In emergency legislation now famously known as the Budget Repair Bill, the governor sought $30 million in concessions from public employees' health and pension benefits and restructured the state's remaining obligations in order to balance the 2011 budget. He also moved to change some provisions of the state's collective bargaining laws to "give state and local governments the tools to manage spending reductions." (Read: to free them from the shackles of public employee unions in order to reduce government waste and redundancy.)

The response to Governor Walker's proposal is now the stuff of political legend.

After the bill passed by a wide margin in the Republican-controlled State House, the Democrat caucus in the State Senate skipped town and holed up in a Red Roof Inn in Illinois to avoid voting on it. Within seventy-two hours, Madison was flooded with busloads of union thugs (oops—members) from the NEA, the SEIU, AFCSME, the UAW, various affiliates of the AFL-CIO, and more, along with what can only be described as a scary collection of Chicago-based communist sympathizers. In fact, every aging hippie with a heartbeat made a beeline for Madison to join the party. Tens of thousands of protestors converged on the state capitol building for the largest and most spirited rallies in decades.

Jesse Jackson and Michael Moore spoke on the capitol steps. Enough said.

Among the most vocal of the protesters were teachers from the Madison and Milwaukee school districts, who staged a union-sponsored four-day "sick out" that cost their districts a combined $6.6 million. According to Wisconsin's McIver Institute, an additional two dozen school districts across the state were forced to close for at least one day due to absent protesting teachers, adding to the burden on the state's beleaguered taxpayers.

Fortunately, proof that the Madison teachers' union was behind the "sick out" meant the school district could exact appropriate penalties. Teachers with unexcused absences were to have their pay docked, but more than a thousand doctor's notes were submitted, many of which were bogus excuses provided by physicians attending the rallies. It will take months, if not years, to determine which teachers will be suspended for submitting false doctor's notes. Meanwhile, there's the pesky issue of educating Madison's children, whose school days were extended for the last quarter of the 2011 school year to make up for the truancy of their teachers.

The size and virulence of the protests were both unsurprising and ultimately ineffective, since the Republicans in the state Senate finally passed the bill without the participation of the missing Democrats. When they did this, protesters stormed the state house and even climbed in through windows when police attempted to close the building, chanting a call and respond cheer:

"Show me what democracy looks like?"

"This is what democracy looks like!"

Had the protesters been educated somewhere besides an American public school, they'd have known this was what *anarchy* looks like. Oh well.

Noteworthy in the Wisconsin protests was the unabashed use of children and teens to advance the campaign of propaganda and misinformation. The Wisconsin protests proved the Left will stop at nothing both to indoctrinate children, and to put them up as a smokescreen to promote a progressive political agenda. Why discuss the real issue of government insolvency when, instead, you can showcase thirteen-year-old Sam Frederick of Wauwatosa standing in front of a sign that reads, "Stop the attack on Wisconsin families," while singing a pro-labor, anti-Walker ballad he wrote "for his teachers." (You can find it on YouTube, but trust me . . . it's painful, mostly because Sam's mother sings along while holding the video camera.)

To be sure, the issue in Wisconsin was never the quality of education for its children—already a dubious reality, especially in the state's urban areas. No, the issue was all about union power, union control, and union privilege. You see, included in the Budget Repair Bill was a provision that the State stop the practice of collecting mandatory dues for public sector unions; and the bill also required that rank and file workers recertify their unions every two years. Given their reaction to the bill, it's possible the unions realize that members will cease forking over union dues if the money is not confiscated from their paychecks.

But this is Wisconsin, the state that prides itself on being the cradle of unionism in America! A place where labor leaders actually refer to themselves as "unionists." In fact, in 2009, former governor Jim Doyle signed into Wisconsin law the Labor History in the Schools bill requiring Wisconsin educators to teach their students the history of collective bargaining.

Every social studies book in America already includes the history of the Triangle Shirtwaist Factory Fire and the subsequent growth of organized labor. So what's the purpose of Wisconsin's law expanding and specifying a labor curriculum?

According to Bryan Kennedy, professor at the University of Wisconsin and president of Wisconsin's chapter of the American Federation of Teachers, it's to indoctrinate children with an eye to *growing the labor movement*. At a 2010 meeting of the Wisconsin Labor History Society that focused on implementing the curriculum law, Kennedy said,

> The topic of today's panel, *How Labor History and Labor Education Can Help Build the Labor Movement*, really is what we need to focus on, and from my perspective in higher Ed, I see that one of the biggest focuses we're going to have as educators in colleges and universities is in teaching teachers what labor unions are about and what collective bargaining is, so that they can teach a curriculum around labor history and collective bargaining to our young people....
>
> What we need to do with this education program is...instill in our young people, and this is only one component of what needs to be a much larger effort, an understanding that America was built on the backs of working people and those working people got ahead because they formed unions and they collectively fought for all the rights that they got in the workplace.... So that as they get older, as they graduate, as they move into the workforce, they're going to be more inclined to recognize that there's a positive aspect to forming a union, in that it gives you a voice in the workplace. Not, wait until conditions get so bad that the only choice that you have left—your last straw [sic]—is to form a union. *We need to change that mentality and the way that happens, really, is by starting this education process at a much younger age and by making it a component of a much larger effort*. But Wisconsin is the first state to do this, so

this is a fledgling effort that starts with us. [emphasis added]

Kennedy makes clear his belief that the role of education is indoctrination, from the college and university level down to elementary students, so that specific beliefs about the benefits of unions are instilled in them.

But what if your state doesn't have a law that requires your children be taught a pro-union curriculum? Never fear, because teachers across the nation often take it upon themselves to weave pro-union messages into the social studies, history, and reading curricula. For example, fifth graders at the Penn Valley Elementary School in the Pennsbury School District of Bucks County, Pennsylvania, were given a reading comprehension assignment made available by a teacher resource company called Teacher Created Materials, Inc. The "Whole Story Comprehension" worksheet included a mock letter to the editor from a fictional eighth grader from Fowlerville, Michigan, in which the writer complains about the "way our teachers are being treated." The letter says, in part:

> We don't pay teachers enough for the very important job they are doing. The average yearly salary for educators in our area is $29,000. As professionals, teachers should be paid like other professionals in our community, such as lawyers and doctors.
>
> Of course, the question isn't, "Why would anyone want to be a teacher?" The real question is, "How could anyone afford to be a teacher—when they are paid such a salary?"
>
> ...I checked with the National Education Association (NEA) and low salaries for educators is [sic] not a problem in just our area. It's happening all over the U.S....

What is the solution? It's simple: raise the salaries of teachers.

Questions that went along with the assignment included a review of the assertions that teachers should be paid like other professionals and that low salaries are a problem in education.

Ready for the punch line? Teachers in the Pennsbury School District were working without a contract at the time this assignment was given to the students, and the issue of teacher salaries was being hotly debated in the community. Also, for the record, the average teacher salary in Pennsbury is $83,000. But let's not confuse the kids.

CHAPTER 6

I PLEDGE ALLEGIANCE TO THE EARTH

In a survey of five hundred American pre-teens commissioned by a kids' environmental web site called HabitatHeros.com, one in three children expressed the belief that the Earth won't even *exist* when they grow up. Overall, the study found 56 percent worry that the planet will be virtually uninhabitable, if not obliterated.

Keep in mind, these are children between the ages of six and eleven. They ought to be afraid of the dark, monsters under their beds, and getting in trouble for not brushing their teeth. Thanks, radicals, for ruining everyone's childhood.

Usually, ignorance is bliss. But in the case of our children's indoctrination by the radical Left, ignorance is also pretty darn convenient. The 2009 National Assessment of Educational Progress (NAEP) science exam showed only one third of American elementary and high school students are minimally proficient in science.

(Only 3 percent scored at the advanced level.) When it comes to science, our kids don't know Newton's apple from apple crisp.

Yet radical Leftists don't think the NAEP score is the science education crisis that must be solved. An April 2011 report from Yale University's Project on Climate Change Communication reveals that only 25 percent of teens passed a seventy-five-question test on climate change. Now *that's* a crisis!

The Yale survey did at least reveal that 57 percent of teens "understand that global warming is caused by human activities" and 71 percent "understand that carbon dioxide is produced by the burning of fossil fuels."

Whew. At least the really important stuff is getting through.

Everybody has to believe in something, and if you're a radical Leftist, more than anything in the world, you believe in the world.

Or more specifically, *The Planet*.

Even more, you believe that human beings are ruining The Planet. But not just any human beings—American citizens of Western heritage, because of our greedy, immoral desire to enjoy a comfortable standard of living.

Earth worship is the secular religion that has replaced theism in the minds and hearts of American radicals. And thanks to their unlimited access to the institutions that influence our children, Leftists are successfully indoctrinating an entire generation of young Americans into the Church of Eco-Centrism.

By hijacking the science curriculum in our public and private schools, and with expert support from our eco-obsessed media, the Left has convinced American children that the Earth is running out of room, out of resources, and out of time. Not surprisingly, they're now suffering from something the Left has labeled "Climate Anxiety" (even worse than "Facebook Depression," the condition kids develop when they realize they have fewer Facebook friends than everyone they know).

Meanwhile, back in the lab, the data that created the notorious "hockey stick"—the graph that "proves" global warming—has all but vanished, and Al Gore & Company have had to recast the whole issue from "global warming" to "Global Climate Change" (GCC) in order to maintain any dignity at all through recent record-setting cold winters.

Common sense is reasserting itself. The folks at Yale, in addition to assessing teen and adult knowledge of climate change, also produced a report called "Global Warming's Six Americas 2010" in which six prevailing attitudes about the subject are tracked. From 2008 to 2010, the group labeled "dismissives" doubled from 8 to 16 percent, while the "alarmed" dropped from 18 to 10 percent. Generally, the groups that previously registered fear are waning while the groups that roll their eyes while stoking up the furnace on a cold night are growing. We all want cheap, renewable energy, which has nothing to do with climate change or treehugging. But I digress.

If the research proves Americans are not quite as worried about the future of our planet as we were a few years ago, it might just be because the science wasn't, in fact, settled. Manipulated? Yes. Fabricated? Certainly. But not necessarily settled. Moreover, most Americans realize that "experts" still can't accurately predict the weather for Saturday's picnic, much less the pattern for hurricanes in the next decade, and apparently no one saw the Japanese tsunami coming until a dozen towns and cities had been washed out to sea.

Yet, Bill Nye the Science Guy, an icon for America's children, appeared on television to claim that the 2011 tornado season, while not mathematically connected to GCC, is *probably* related to it—but only in the U.S.A. (Never mind La Niña, which climatologists on all sides of the issue agree is the cause of the record-breaking storm season of 2011. Whatever, Science Guy.)

I must be scientifically inclined because I'm a huge skeptic. Isn't that one of the prerequisites?

Anyway, if the science about GCC remains in debate at least in some circles, it most certainly is not questioned by the National Science Teachers Association (NSTA), which offers myriad professional development seminars to help America's teachers of science share alarmism about GCC with their students. At the 2010 national NSTA conference, presentations included "Global Climate change as a Theme for Teaching Science," in which researchers from Florida Atlantic University described "research [that] focuses on developing and piloting two instruments that measure elementary methods students' (preservice and practicing teachers') knowledge and attitudes about GCC at the beginning and end of a science methods course, as well as developing and implementing an instructional intervention."

Though the sample size was small, this research demonstrates the insidious manner in which so-called climate science is being brought to America's classrooms:

> We begin our instruction by having students [of the Department of Education] view *An Inconvenient Truth*, the Al Gore documentary regarding global warming. The film illustrates typical topics taught in a science methods course (i.e., processes of science and the nature of science). Students analyze the evidence Gore used to support his explanations of GCC in the film. Interestingly, most students have not seen the film and are moved by the visuals and information presented in the film.

During most viewings one could hear a pin drop as the film proceeds. The majority of students report increased or new interest in GCC as the result of watching the film, and many acquire the DVD for home viewing and for repeat viewing. In a recent small intense summer class, only one student out of 13 reported no increased interest in GCC as a result of watching the film, while the other 12 found the documentary changed the way they viewed the world and the choices they might make in their daily lives. They reported that they were deeply affected by the content of the film.

Advancing the theme of GCC continued at the most recent NSTA national conference in March 2011, where the eleven thousand-plus educators in attendance were able not only to find the materials and lesson plans they need to teach GCC to their kindergarteners-through-high-schoolers, but also were motivated and inspired to do it.

Among the national speakers on hand, NSTA's keynote was delivered by the notable Jeff Goldstein, Ph.D., Director of the National Center for Earth and Space Science Education (NCESSE), an organization funded by the Tides Center (Soros!), as well as Eugenie C. Scott, executive director of the National Center for Science Education, an organization founded in 1981 for the purpose of advancing atheism by keeping intelligent design out of America's public schools. (Oops! I mean, founded to improve and support the teaching of evolution.)

I'll extrapolate a bit here, but see if it makes sense: American students are measurably and woefully undereducated in the sciences. At the same time, they have high levels of anxiety about Global Climate Change as well as some strongly held beliefs about how GCC is caused and about its potential for the destruction of our earth in the near future. Meanwhile, science education appears to have been commandeered for greater political purposes (obviously not to teach actual science) while in support of the GCC gospel, the entertainment media advance the simplistic values that define radical Leftism.

Kool-Aid, flowing like a river.

There Really Is a Pledge

Of all the truly obnoxious ways in which children are plied with eco-radicalism, an especially insidious one is the "Earth Pledge," recited regularly in a few schools, but widely on Earth Day. Couched in lovely phrases about peace and harmony, the Pledge undercuts patriotism (pledge your allegiance to the earth, not to a flag or the country it stands for), equates all life forms, advocates redistribution of resources, and articulates the vision of a utopian world—all in one tidy, memorable parody of the pledge to the American flag:

> I pledge allegiance to the earth, and to all life that it nourishes;
>
> All growing things, all species of animals, and all races of people.
>
> I promise to protect all life on our planet, to live in harmony in nature, and to share our resources justly, so that all people can live in dignity, good health and in peace.

The text of the Earth Pledge synopsizes the Left's eco-platform in a nutshell. (Not to mention the United Nations' goals, as illustrated by a recent UN proposal pitched by Bolivia that will give "Mother Earth" the same rights as human beings. Too weird to discuss.)

America's science curriculum is being thoroughly bastardized not only to promote eco-centrism, but also to undermine free market capitalism. In her handbook for educators, *Teaching Science for Social Justice*, Michigan State University professor Angela Calabrese-Barton explains:

> The marriages between capitalism and education and capitalism and science have created a foundation for science education that emphasizes corporate values at the expense of social justice and human dignity.... Science pedagogy framed around social justice concerns can become a *medium to transform individuals, schools, communities, the environment, and science itself,* in ways that promote equity and social justice. Creating a science education that is transformative implies not only how *science is a political activity* but also the ways in which students might see and use science and science education in ways transformative of the institutional and interpersonal power structures that play a role in their lives. [emphasis added]

Cool. Let's transform *science itself* to achieve our political objectives! And the Left has the audacity to accuse conservatives of being anti-science. By the way, Calabrese-Barton's book is part of a series published by Teachers College Press called Teaching for Social Justice. The series editor? Bill Ayers.

When it comes to instilling the values of eco-radicalism, Al Gore remains a guru for science teachers across the nation. *An Inconvenient*

Truth has been shown in thousands of U.S. schools and the film's production company, Participant Media, offers a downloadable curriculum guide as well. In fact, free lesson plans are available all over the Internet, from groups such as climatecrisis.net (the film's home page) to the National Wildlife Federation, from Britannica to the Ohio Education Association.

Just don't try to get any lesson plans from the United Kingdom. After the British government's Department for Children, Schools, and Families sent free copies of *An Inconvenient Truth* to every school in Britain, including Scotland and Wales, a school board member in Kent sued over the film's lopsided portrayal of the environmental debate. A British judge ruled the film contains nine major "errors of fact" that are so glaring, Al Gore's movie may no longer be presented in British classrooms as scientifically based without an appropriate disclaimer and the airing of opposing points of view.

Fortunately, here in the States we don't worry about that sort of thing—especially when a video can chew up one or two class periods.

Then again, you can't keep playing Al Gore's magnum opus over and over again. Enter *Human Footprint*, a 2008 production from National Geographic on the impact of consumption—specifically that of U.S. citizens—on the environment.

According to National Geographic, the film uses "science and revelatory visual events" to deliver "an extraordinary personal audit of how much of the world's resources each of us consumes, illustrating the average American's human footprint."

You're probably wondering what a "revelatory visual event" is. Essentially it's another way to say "images that are meant to shock and shame you." Such as, for example, a massive American flag created from the 4,476 loaves of bread each of us will consume in a lifetime, an assemblage of 28,443 rubber ducks to represent the showers we will take while using 700,000 gallons of water, and a forklift dropping 19,826 eggs to create a disgusting, yolk-soaked symbol for the omelets and devilled eggs we will eat before we die.

Of course, the purpose of *Human Footprint* isn't just to create awareness of consumption. Its true aim is to convict Americans of the social sin of living in an affluent nation. There's even a teacher's guide available online to help instructors convey this message: "By their first birthday, the average American will be responsible for more carbon dioxide emissions than a person in Tanzania generates in a lifetime."

Ann McElhinney, co-creator of the documentary *Not Evil Just Wrong*, which challenges much of the "settled science" about global warming and climate change, says the message behind "educational" films such as *Human Footprint* is nothing more than propaganda.

"It is not only disingenuous, but also shabby education, not to point out that, according to the World Health Organization, average life expectancy in the U.S. is 78.4 years and rising, while that number is as low as 48 years in Tanzania," McElhinney says. "It is unconscionable for anyone to fail to point out also that in Tanzania more than one in 10 children die before their fifth birthday, not from carbon dioxide emissions or climate change, but mostly from preventable conditions such as diarrhea (17%), malaria (23%), and pneumonia (21%). I think any self-respecting educator ought to point that out...

"All over the U.S., schools are using films produced by groups like the World Wildlife Fund, the Sierra Club and the Tides Foundation that all tell essentially the same story: America is bad, consumerism is bad, capitalism bad and the human footprint is bad," McElhinney points out. "This film also challenges children to come up with ways to counter all that bad behavior, including references to population control."

Apparently these lessons are too important to leave up to science teachers—some of them may not be inspired to act as Leftist purveyors of eco-agitprop. No, only the U.S. Department of Education is big enough and bold enough to ensure the environmentalist message gets into every classroom. Thus Secretary of Education Arne Duncan in September 2010 declared at something called the Sustainability Education Summit: Citizenship and Pathways for a Green Economy, "Right now, in the second decade of the twenty-first century, preparing our children to be good environmental citizens is some of the most important work any of us can do. It's work that will serve future generations—and quite literally sustain our world."

"Historically," Duncan said, "the Department of Education hasn't been doing enough to drive the sustainability movement, and today, I promise that we will be a committed partner in the national effort to build a more environmentally literate and responsible society. I want my department to help advance the sustainability movement through education." To this end, Duncan vowed that his department would provide federally subsidized school programs beginning as early as kindergarten that teach children about climate change and prepare them "to contribute to the workforce through green jobs."

Way to go, Arne. That ought to help boost our test scores. Or maybe not.

Eco-radicals at the House of Mouse

If the American school curriculum is not yet as eco-centric as Secretary Duncan or the radical Left would prefer, never fear. Our children absorb an average of seven and a half hours of media per day, much of which expounds upon and supports the eco-radical themes introduced in their shoddy pseudo-science classes.

As we know, when the Leftist media machine mobilizes, it is capable of producing a slick, appealing, and progressive entertainment product, and thus can easily indoctrinate an unsuspecting audience of impressionable children.

The Left loves to speak directly to America's children about civic pride and participation. And when they do, they seem perfectly patriotic. Yet programming and entertainment for children is like a connect-the-dots picture. Once you finish drawing the lines, you can see the progressive politics at the heart of it all.

Nowhere is this strategy more evident than in Disney's "Friends for Change" and Nickelodeon's "The Big Help" programs.

Disney employs the full resources of the House of Mouse to indoctrinate children into radical eco-Leftism. Built around the network's stable of tween stars, Friends for Change's "Project Green" brings together all aspects of a sophisticated multimedia advertising campaign with public service announcements on the Disney Channel and Radio Disney, along with an interactive website. Young actors and singers from the network's hottest shows encourage children to get involved and become informed, and they even have a theme song: "Make a Wave" ("just a pebble in the water, ooh, can set the sea in motion, ooh..."). It's *Mickey Mouse Club* meets Al Gore.

Friends for Change has two main goals: to promote small alterations in daily habits that supposedly will "help the planet," and to involve child participants in Disney's distribution of $1 million each year for environmental activism by allowing them to vote on their favorite projects.

The small changes Disney encourages are the sorts of things you'd expect—turning off the water while brushing your teeth or washing dishes, riding a bike instead of taking a car to the park, taking shorter showers and not using the toilet as a trash can to avoid more frequent flushing. (If you had to read that last one twice, you're not alone. I did too.) Thanks to Friends for Change, an entire generation of children may grow up to believe that cleaning the lint filter in the clothes drier is an act of community service, but whatever.

The more insidious indoctrination is found in the projects Disney funds, and especially in the manner in which they describe those initiatives to children. It's clear that Disney's enviro-dollars are meant to offset the impact of greedy and evil humans, whose very existence threatens wildlife and habitats around the globe. But not to worry, because Disney's eco-partner organizations are here to save the day! (It almost sounds like the plot of a movie. Oh wait! It is!)

A quick click of the computer mouse will take kids from the Disney website to the World Wildlife Fund's site, where they will discover that "Almost a quarter of the world's mammals face a high risk of extinction within 30 years."

Over at Fauna & Flora International's web site (fauna-flora.org), children can learn that "The best information that science can provide suggests that species are disappearing at a rate between 1,000 and 10,000 times higher than it would naturally be, with the prospect that 50% of all current life forms may ultimately be lost." And at the Natural Resources Defense Council's "Biogems" site (savebiogems.org), children will have their suspicions about greedy, evil humans confirmed: "Now more than ever, North and South America's last wildlands and rarest wildlife are under threat from large scale logging, mining and industrialization."

Meanwhile, hundreds of thousands of children in Africa are at risk of dying this year alone from the entirely preventable disease of malaria, which, with the safe and effective use of DDT, could be eradicated before today's Disney star is old enough to play a grownup on TV. But in Africa, Disney is using its considerable resources to help protect elephant paths.

Nickelodeon is equally committed to the cause of environmentalism, and also promotes it under the banner of "service." But Nickelodeon goes even further down the road of progressive activism. Here's a statement from its website, pro-social.nick.com: "The Big Help is Nickelodeon's pro-social campaign with the mission of engaging kids to make a difference in the world by moving their bodies, minds, communities, and planet." Initiatives and resources are focused on four areas: environment, health and wellness, education, and community.

Does that strike you, as it does me, as an awfully broad mission?

The Big Help's big umbrella of initiatives is big by design. By extending itself across a variety of areas, Nickelodeon is free to promote a wide array of progressive, politically correct messages directly to children, with assistance from online "partners," including Michelle Obama's "Let's Move" campaign, the NEA, the National Environmental Education Association, the Natural Resources Defense Fund, the United Nations Environment Programme (UNEP), and Get Schooled, a coordinated effort between Viacom and the Bill & Melinda Gates Foundation.

The Big Help website invites children to join its social networking community and then earn points by making commitments to various "pro-social" activities. The points take you through various levels of participation, from "citizen" to "advocate" to "activist" to "champion." I joined to see what it's like to be a Big Helper, so to speak. Starting in the "environment space" (so I can help change the world!), I earned fifty points by promising to ask my family to buy CFL light bulbs and reading the directions telling me how to change them. (Short answer: ask a grownup.)

I earned another forty points for promising to learn about the BP oil spill by visiting the National Wildlife Federation's site at nfw.org/oil_spill/kids. There, I read that some people hold BP responsible for the spill, while others think the government is at least partly to blame, but really, "you could say that all of us play a part: people all over the world keep demanding—and using—more and more oil. That means more and more oil has to be found and pumped out of the ground. That can be harmful to the Earth even where drilling is easy. But the 'easy' oil is almost all gone, so oil companies have to go to places where drilling becomes very risky— like in the deep waters of the Gulf." In the spirit of Rahm Emanuel, NWF answered the question, "What can I do to keep from feeling sad and worried about what's happening?" with this upbeat response: "Environmental disasters truly are tough on us, on wild creatures, and the wild places we all love and need. But it often takes things like this to make us do what's right. So let's not let this one go to waste!"

These child-friendly sites all convey the Leftist myth that we're running out of oil, that fossil fuels are bad, and that we have to change our way of life and use less energy. And don't forget, the BP oil spill was *our* fault.

Another task, voting on the names for two baby gorillas, took me to the UNEP site, where I found another list of easy ways to help save the environment. The best one I won't do: "When deciding what you're going to eat for the day, go vegan once a week. Many people may not know this, but raising animals for food generates a considerable amount of greenhouse gases!"

Nickelodeon also operates a separate site for The Big Green Help, teaching children politically correct lessons about climate change and radical environmentalism through interactive, online games and a child-friendly social networking platform. The "five elements" of the Big Green Help include reducing the use of energy, recycling and "precycling" (don't ask, I have no clue), reducing CO_2 in the Earth's atmosphere, curbing the use of automobiles, and using less water ("Water is also a precious resource that humans use too much of"). A Big Green Quiz ensures that children know the right answers to questions such as, "Because the temperature of the earth's surface is getting warmer, which of the following is true?" The correct answer: "More than 20% of the Polar ice cap has melted away." Not that that's debatable or anything.

Moving to The Big Help's "health and wellness space," I could earn points by getting eight hours of sleep, eating together with my family, brushing my teeth twice a day, drinking water, playing sports, and participating in Nickelodeon's World Wide Day of Play. That's the day that Nickelodeon and its sister networks suspend programming for three hours from noon until 3 p.m. and post a message on-screen telling young viewers to get off the couch and go outdoors. I earned so many points on that one, I'm an "advocate" now.

But what does all this have to do with "helping"? It's a good idea to brush your own teeth, and I suppose you could view it as a service to your loved ones, but it's not exactly the stuff of altruism or philanthropy. And the brand of volunteerism that the Left promotes to children is nothing but progressive political activism. Both Disney's Friends for Change and Nickelodeon's The Big Help claim millions of youthful participants. And it's clear that the agendas of "pro-social" programs such as these are ultimately just "pro-socialist."

But never fear. Once the kids outgrow their interest in the citizenship lessons of Disney and Nickelodeon, they can flip the dial to MTV, where, in addition to lots of soft-core porn, they'll find out how to "Rock the Vote."

Love the Environment but Hate the Humans (Especially Capitalists!): Agitprop for the Whole Family

It's simply not possible to document all of the Left's influence over children through America's entertainment media. By the time I finish writing this chapter, someone will have yelled, "Cut!" on yet another production meant to inspire kids to radical environmental action or a life of anti-capitalist crusades, and already I'll have left something out. My overview is necessarily incomplete. The point isn't to ferret out and dissect every Leftist media property, but to help conservatives identify the propaganda and respond appropriately. (Often: "Turn that thing off.") But some of these TV shows and movies are wonderful entertainment! Just because there's a political message lurking in the subtext doesn't mean we can't enjoy the shows, but we ought to use them as openings for conversations with the children in our spheres of influence.

What follows, then, are just a few examples of how the Left skews family-friendly entertainment for progressive, politically correct purposes.

From1942's *Bambi* to 2003's *Finding Nemo*, Disney has for generations influenced the ways in which children view the natural world. That's not necessarily a bad thing when the message is to respect nature and all the living creatures in it—including the people. But clearly, many of the current films for kids are meant to instill radical environmentalist values.

In *The Idea of Nature in Disney Animation*, Cambridge University lecturer David Whitley points out that many green activists say *Bambi* inspired their interest in conservation and "laid the emotional groundwork for environmental activism." (Possibly no one explained to these folks it was just a cartoon.) Given that Disney animator Ollie Johnston, who inked *Bambi*, asked that upon his death he be remembered by donations to the Natural Resources Defense Council, it's likely this outcome was intended.

Finding Nemo promotes not only environmentalism but also veganism, as when Bruce the shark announces: "I am a nice shark, not a mindless eating machine. If I am to change this image, I must first change myself. Fish are friends, not food." Being nice means not eating animals. Got that?

For sheer anti-human, anti-capitalist propaganda, there's no better children's movie than the 1992 animated film *Fern Gully: The Last Rainforest*. In this PC kiddie primer, a fairy named Crysta and her family live peacefully under the rainforest canopy until she learns from a blind bat about some horrible creatures called "humans" who are out to destroy their homes by "logging." When Crysta befriends a young employee of the logging company, she finds an ally (for enviro-terrorism). A recent review by a green blogger mom said that when the film first came out, parents were up in arms about the message that humans are destroying the earth, but, "Personally I feel that it might just be reality slapping us in the face. My kids and I love this movie and it is great for introducing your kids to the cause of environmentalism in a way they can understand."

The 2005 film *Over the Hedge* tells the tale of animals who awaken from hibernation to find their forest half gone because of (guess who?) more loggers. *TV Guide* called it "a sly satire of American 'enough is never enough' consumerism and blind progress at the expense of the environment." Do kids get satire? Hard to say. They do get bad cinema, though; a gag where a bear knocks over a guy in a port-a-john is too predictable even for children.

In 2006, *Happy Feet* switched the focus from logging to fishing (but not away from the evil humans). This story about a penguin that dances but can't sing offers an endearing and unlikely hero that kids just love. An online review said the film "clinches the current trend of animated message films that speak for the plight of animals and the ecology.... Mumble and his pals survive attacks from sea lions and killer whales, but it is mankind's ruthless fishing around their home of Antarctica that threatens to wipe out all of the area's wildlife. Mumble must go on a personal journey to bring the plight of the penguins to the world."

The message of radical environmentalism makes for both bad and good films. For example, the 2010 film *Furry Vengeance* was panned—but not because it depicted a developer as evil and raccoons who behave like eco-terrorists as good, but because it boasted a bad script, lame gags, gross humor, and lousy computer-generated animals. Of course, that hasn't stopped the Leftist activist organization Participant Media from building a social justice campaign around this film. Founded in 2004, Participant Media's mission is "to entertain audiences first, then to invite them to participate in making a difference." (Agitprop? Nah...) This is the group responsible for bringing Al Gore's *An Inconvenient Truth* into classrooms nationwide. Now, Participant aims to indoctrinate children with this wacky comedy starring B-listers Brooke Shields and Brendan Fraser.

I don't know about you, but if my kids are going to endure Leftist propaganda in the classroom, I think it should at least be well done. For excellence in Leftism, the award goes to...James Cameron's *Avatar*.

Avatar, released just in time for the 2009 Christmas movie season (who says Cameron isn't a capitalist?), is the epic science fiction film set in the year 2054 on the distant moon Pandora, home of the willowy Na'vi, a tribe of 10-foot-tall, blue-skinned humanoids who live in harmony with their surroundings and worship the goddess Eywa. In the midst of this lush environment, an American company called RDA mines the mineral unobtanium (get it?), unceremoniously raping the land as it goes—while, of course, the U.S. military protects RDA because of national security interests. The story follows a disabled former marine named Jake Sully on his redemptive journey as he is transformed into an avatar—a human-Na'vi hybrid—who learns the error of his human, militarist, capitalist, American ways. Sully becomes the heroic figure whose prayers to Eywa result in the defeat of the U.S. military, RDA, and all things American.

How good is *Avatar's* agitprop? *Popular Science's* review said, "Cameron reaches for a heavy environmental message. *Avatar* is every militant global warming supporter's dream come true as the invading, technology-worshiping, environment-ravaging humans are set upon by an angry planet and its noble inhabitants."

But the movie's entertainment value went beyond its message. Writing in *The Christian Post*, Russell D. Moore, Dean of the School of Theology at the Southern Baptist Theological Seminary, said, "If you can get a theater full of people in Kentucky to stand and applaud the defeat of their country in war, then you've got some amazing special effects."

But even if miners in Kentucky applauded Cameron's film, not everyone did. Ann McElhinney, who in addition to *Not Evil Just Wrong* directed the documentary *Mine Your Own Business*, declared *Avatar* 162 minutes of Left-wing garbage. Speaking at 2010's Conservative Political Action Conference, she said, "Unfortunately, you have to see it. It is beautiful...it's compelling...you nearly at the end are hoping the Americans die, but it is *rubbish*. It's unbelievable rubbish. It's an anti-American, anti-capitalist, anti-mining rant, and it is rubbish. And every child in this country is going to see it."

If not every child, darn near. One way to assess a movie such as this is simply to note that it has earned $2.740 *billion* worldwide. Within forty-seven days of its release, *Avatar* became the highest grossing film of all time in Canada and the U.S., a distinction it later earned in at least thirty other countries. In North American theaters alone, it is estimated that 75 million tickets were sold, more than to any other film since 1999's *Star Wars Episode I: The Phantom Menace*.

Meanwhile, though Cameron has been quoted as saying that enormous wealth makes him uncomfortable and "greed tends to destroy the environment," he's not above indulging in a little capitalistic cross-marketing. Leftist groups criticized him for partnering with McDonald's to promote *Avatar*, despite a 2006 Greenpeace report that said McDonald's is partly to blame for deforestation of rainforests (apparently they use soybeans grown in rainforest regions for animal feed). Hypocrisy, thy name is Cameron.

But as *Popular Science* noted, hypocrisy lies at the heart of *Avatar*:

> The film's message suffers mightily under the weight of mind-boggling hypocrisy. Cameron's story clearly curses the proliferation of human technology. In *Avatar*, the science and machinery of humankind leads to soulless violence and destruction. It only serves to pollute the primitive but pristine paradise of Pandora. Of course, without centuries of development in science and technology, the film putting forth this simple-minded, self-loathing worldview wouldn't exist. You'd imagine Cameron himself would be bored to tears on the planet he created. There are no movies on Pandora, so he'd be out of a job. The Na'vi rarely visit a multiplex. They sit around their glowing trees, chanting; they don't build and sink titanic ocean liners, and they don't construct deep-sea mini-subs enabling certain filmmakers to spend countless days exploring said cruise ships.

Movie review as political exposé? Absolutely.

CHAPTER 7

LAND OF THE FREE, HOME OF THE MULTI-CULTURALLY DIVERSE

According to a study by the Arthur Levitt Public Affairs Center at New York's Hamilton College, a plurality of American young adults believe that legal immigrants, even though they aren't American citizens, should be allowed to vote in American elections. According to the eighteen- to twenty-nine-year-olds surveyed, the government should do more to integrate illegal immigrants, and less to enforce immigration laws. The survey found younger people markedly more open to government policies that make it easier for foreigners to enter the United States. The report was entitled, "Immigration and Racial Change: Are All Generations on the Same Page?"

No, as a matter of fact, they're not: "Younger Americans are consistently more open to multiculturalism than their older counterparts...."

The Left's campaign to change America's values about citizenship has not been for nothing. Our children have been taught they are "global citizens" first—and they're taking that lesson to heart.

When radical Leftists talk about "fundamentally transforming the United States of America," as Barack Obama did just five days before he was elected to the presidency, they're not just referring to the changes they wish to implement in our systems and institutions. They're talking about replacing our American character with an entirely different national ethos.

Since their aim is to promote the evolution of our nation-state from one kind of America ("jingoistic") to another (global!), they must do more than achieve electoral, legislative, and regulatory victory. They don't want only to impose Leftism from the top down. No, they have to mold the hearts and minds of our citizens, and especially the hearts and minds of our youngest citizens. They have to make our children reject our heritage and instead expect and want their new, improved America.

Score one more for the Left.

Across the institutions with the greatest influence on our children's attitudes and beliefs, the radical Left is successfully undermining our American character by teaching our children that patriotism is simply wrong. There's nothing exceptional about America, remember. It's narrow-minded and prejudiced to think that there is. Multiculturalism alone represents the most noble moral world view. Global citizenship is the goal.

There is probably not a school system, college, university, or organization in America that does not have a formal policy on multiculturalism, with most claiming diversity as a "core belief." Driven by the desire to eradicate discrimination and the assumption that political correctness is now the law of the land, schools and organizations have become pawns in a high stakes game of political maneuvering. The spoils in this battle? The voters of tomorrow.

Of course openness to and acceptance of people from all racial and ethnic backgrounds represents an extraordinary opportunity for national unity. America has long been a nation of immigrants. *E pluribus unum*—"Out of many, one"—is the motto on the Seal of the United States. And it's not a good thing, but a *great* thing, that our children are the most color-blind cohort of Americans—in part, because of their generation's own multi-ethnic makeup. Census projections indicate more than half of all babies born in the U.S. are minorities and that we will be a minority-majority country by 2030.

But traditional American "out of many, one"-style national unity is not what the Left has in mind for the United States. They're more about "divide and conquer."

As unpopular and politically incorrect as this statement will seem, "multiculturalism" is eroding our American character. Our nation's children, rather than inheriting a stronger, freer America, are being sold a bill of goods about what's really best for our country. The multiculturalism and "diversity" our kids are taught in school are undermining the healthy process of assimilation that turned previous waves of immigrants into patriotic American citizens who embraced the values, virtues, and habits that caused this country to flourish.

Thanks to school-based cultural training and widespread political correctness, America's young people believe the twenty-first-century platitude, "our strength is our diversity." Too bad it's not actually true.

In 2007, Harvard political scientist Robert Putnam, author of the national bestseller *Bowling Alone: The Collapse and Revival of American Community*, released (albeit reluctantly) the results of a massive study of thirty thousand people from forty-one communities and cities and concluded exactly the opposite: our diversity makes us weaker. Specifically, this largest-ever study on civic engagement in America found that by virtually all measures, civic engagement is lower in more diverse communities. (Putnam, a Leftist academic, struggled to find ways to refine the research so that it might show a different result, as he apparently was horrified to realize that diversity didn't help communities to be more engaged. Poor guy. Must have been a shock to his system.)

Putnam's findings refuted two popular ideas about the impact of diversity—"contact" and "conflict"—that is, that people in highly diverse communities will naturally form bonds with people from other races and cultures because of frequent contact, or that living in diverse communities will create racial and ethnic conflict. Apparently neither one actually tends to happen. Instead, Putnam discovered that in conditions of "diversity" people become "turtles," retreating into their shells. Not exactly a recipe for civic engagement.

Diversity over assimilation as a "core value" not only weakens our society. It specifically also shortchanges immigrant children—denying them access to the very opportunities that immigrants seek when they make their way to our shores. Diane Ravitch, professor of education at New York University and former assistant Secretary of Education in the George W. Bush administration, wrote in a 2002 Brookings Institution article,

> A democratic society must seek to give every young person, whether native-born or newcomer, the knowledge and skills to succeed as an adult. In a political system that relies on the participation of informed citizens, everyone should, at a minimum, learn to speak, read, and write a common language. Those who would sustain our democratic life must understand its history. To maximize their

ability to succeed in the future, young people must also learn mathematics and science. Tailoring children's education to the color of their skin, their national origins, or their presumed ethnicity is in some fundamental sense contrary to our nation's founding ideals of democracy, equality, and opportunity.

Ravitch says assimilation alone isn't appropriate because diversity adds depth and richness to the fabric of our American culture. "But neither is 'celebrating diversity' an adequate strategy for a multiracial, multi-ethnic society like ours. The public schools exist to build an American community, to help both newcomers and native-born children prepare for adulthood as fellow citizens." The political correctness of diversity as a core value essentially cheats some children out of their right to be fully engaged in American society.

Of course, merely suggesting any of this will get me branded a racist in no time flat, because that's what the Left does whenever they're confronted with the hypocrisy and disingenuousness of their orchestrated effort to marginalize (sorry, celebrate) "diverse" peoples. (I'm already a "bastard" according to the NEA's former general counsel, Bob Chanin. Whatever.)

But the truth is, the multicultural movement, especially as presented in our educational institutions, isn't really about fostering greater respect among people of different racial and ethnic backgrounds. It's about building the self-esteem of certain ethnic groups while shaming those who have the audacity to prefer a distinct American culture. And most of all, it's about manipulating the expectations of an entire generation so they'll abandon our nation's heritage of American exceptionalism and benevolent hegemony and instead go marching into the glorious sunset of our republican form of government toward unambitious, unmotivated, uninspired, unexceptional socialism.

The way this works in practice is truly absurd. For example, there's the case of young Cody Alicea, a thirteen-year-old student at Denair Middle School near Sacramento, California. For several months at the start of the 2010 academic year, Cody rode his bike to school with an American flag affixed to his rear fender. When he arrived at school each day, he'd lock his ride at the bike rack and then neatly and respectfully fold his flag and put it in his backpack until the end of the day, when he replaced it for his patriotic ride home.

Inexplicably in November, school administrators told him to stop putting Old Glory on his bike and instead leave the flag at home. They didn't want to inflame "racial tensions." Apparently, the school's Hispanic students didn't appreciate Cody's display of patriotism, and officials feared trouble was brewing. Ultimately, after his parents and grandparents complained (dad and grandpa are veterans, by the way), the superintendent of schools admitted that Cody's First Amendment rights included the right to fly the flag of our nation while riding his bike to a public building, financed by California taxpayers, where on the lawn in front of the school the Stars and Stripes are flown each day.

In retrospect, Cody should have known better. Earlier in the year in Morgan Hill, California, five students at Live Oak High School were reprimanded on Cinco de Mayo for wearing American flag t-shirts to school. The principal explained that their show of American patriotism was "offensive" to students of Mexican heritage on what was meant to be "their special day."

I have no words for that one—which is inconvenient in a book.

Meanwhile, Back at the Mosque

Not only is it offensive to be jingoistically patriotic (apparently there's no other way to do it), but it is also xenophobic to question the wisdom or value of multicultural studies. In fact, when radical Leftists overtly infuse anti-Western ideas into the school curriculum, there should be nary a peep of objection.

For example, in May 2010, middle schoolers from Wellesley, Massachusetts, visited the Islamic Society of Boston Community Center as part of a course called "Enduring Beliefs in the World Today." A parent who chaperoned the trip took a video on her phone, and that video was released months later by Americans for Peace and Tolerance, an organization that monitors the Boston Islamic Center. The video shows a Muslim woman explaining to girls why Islam and Allah do not marginalize females, and later, removing all the women to the rear of the facility when the call for prayer is sounded. Then the video captures five sixth-grade boys, all non-Muslims, joining in Islamic prayers with the men of the Center. On a *public school field trip*, it must be restated.

Only after the video went viral on the Internet did Wellesley School Superintendent Bella Wong send a letter of apology to parents. It took four months and a link on the Drudge Report for Wong to finally admit that allowing the children to participate in the prayer service was a mistake.

Imagine the uproar from the ACLU if the field trip had been to Boston's Cathedral of the Holy Cross and a handful of non-Catholic students had knelt before the altar? Or if the "enduring tradition" being viewed was full-immersion baptism at a Christian church and a student who hadn't been raised a Christian had just happened to jump into the warm waters of redemption?

The uncomfortable reality is, the diversity agenda isn't about honoring and cherishing all racial, ethnic, and religious traditions. It's about apologizing for our Western, Judeo-Christian foundations while pretending not to notice that we're elevating in the eyes of our children the very cultures that hold America in disdain.

After so much Kool-Aid being mainlined into the veins and brains of our children, some people are fighting back. Case in point: Arizona. Admittedly, Arizona could be the example for countless efforts to preserve and protect American citizenship and culture. But specifically, Arizona's legislation to ban ethnic studies classes such as the Tucson Unified School District's (TUSD) Raza Studies class.

In the mainstream media, the TUSD Raza Studies controversy seemed to boil down to nobly defiant Mexican-Americans who wanted to teach a culturally and racially relevant curriculum fighting against an O.W.R.G. (Old White Republican Guy) who felt threatened by the demographic realities of our porous border. Political correctness and the "core value" of diversity made it nearly impossible to find objective stories about the actual content of the Raza Studies course. Unless you looked high and low for substantive coverage of the controversy, the enactment of the legislation on ethnic studies—closely following, as it did, Arizona's illegal immigration enforcement law—looked like just one more example of Governor Jan Brewer's obvious anti-Mexican prejudice.

Or not.

In fact, the TUSD Raza Studies controversy began in 2006 when Dolores Huerta, co-founder with Cesar Chavez of the United Farm Workers, spoke at Tucson High School and told students, among other things, that there was no reason why America could not be as wonderful as Venezuela, where President Hugo Chavez had built factories for "the people" to work in, as well as hospitals in every neighborhood so "the people" could be treated for free. She decried capitalism as only benefiting rich whites and most memorably said, "Republicans hate Latinos." I've heard the audio. It's not very nice.

State School Superintendent Tom Horne, now Arizona Attorney General, was offended. According to the mainstream media, of course, his objection was only to Huerta's comment about Republicans. You'd never guess from the news coverage that Horne's objection had to do with the fact that the Raza Studies course taught anti-American, anti-capitalist, anti-Western bigotry on the public dime.

So Superintendent Horne spearheaded what the Left calls a radical, racist law to ban such a curriculum from the state's classrooms. But you have to ask yourself who is radical and racist in this fight? Here are the main provisions of Arizona House Bill 2281:

THE LEGISLATURE FINDS AND DECLARES THAT PUBLIC SCHOOL PUPILS SHOULD BE TAUGHT TO TREAT AND VALUE EACH OTHER AS INDIVIDUALS AND NOT BE TAUGHT TO RESENT OR HATE OTHER RACES OR CLASSES OF PEOPLE.

A. A SCHOOL DISTRICT OR CHARTER SCHOOL IN THIS STATE SHALL NOT INCLUDE IN ITS PROGRAM OF INSTRUCTION ANY COURSES OR CLASSES THAT INCLUDE ANY OF THE FOLLOWING:

1. PROMOTE THE OVERTHROW OF THE UNITED STATES GOVERNMENT.

2. PROMOTE RESENTMENT TOWARD A RACE OR CLASS OF PEOPLE.

3. ARE DESIGNED PRIMARILY FOR PUPILS OF A PARTICULAR ETHNIC GROUP.

4. ADVOCATE ETHNIC SOLIDARITY INSTEAD OF THE TREATMENT OF PUPILS AS INDIVIDUALS.

Heck, if the Raza Studies folks in Arizona think this law is bad, just imagine how they feel about legislation signed into law in March 2011 in Utah. In House Bill 220, the Utah legislature actually mandated that pupils learn that our form of government is a compound constitutional republic, and not a democracy. The law specifies that students undergo "thorough study" of our founding documents, our national motto, and the Pledge of Allegiance. They're even requiring that students learn the difference between individualism, socialism, and free market capitalism.

What next, Utah? Phonics?

The backlash expressed in these two states may reflect a quiet uprising against political correctness in our classrooms. In a March 2010 Rasmussen poll, "Sixty percent of Americans with children in elementary or secondary school say most school textbooks are more concerned with presenting information in a politically correct manner than in accuracy."

Making textbooks more accurate and less politically correct is no small task. Just ask the folks on the Texas Board of Education, where conservatives who in 2010 fought for more balanced language in history and social studies texts were accused of attempting to infuse textbooks with Right-wing propaganda. Mary Beth Berlanga, a longtime Texas board member and Hispanic activist, was quoted in the *New York Times* as saying, "They are rewriting history. They can just pretend this is a white America and Hispanics don't exist."

But Gilbert Sewell, director of the non-partisan non-profit American Textbook Council (ATC), wrote in the *Washington Post* about the Texas controversy,

> The hearings and their aftermath showcase a profound gulf over public interpretation of history in schools. It also indicates that any deviation from multicultural convention will provoke violent reaction and criticism.
>
> In too many classrooms, and this has been true for a good quarter century, enslaved Africans, exterminated

Indians, oppressed women, exploited immigrants and minorities, all discriminated against, some interred in concentration camps, comprise the American narrative. Was Truman a war criminal? Let's put him on trial in class.

Revisionists expect a classroom monopoly and exclusive interpretive rights to history. They do not want a balanced history and never have, but as historian Gary Nash once said, a redistribution of historical capital.

In social studies and across the curriculum, the diversity industry calls the tune—the only tune—in publishers' editorial offices, and has for a long time. Diversity is locked into the textbook system. So when conservatives fight back, all hell breaks loose.

Funny, the Left only thinks textbooks contain propaganda when the content goes counter to their political purposes. For example, no one on the Left seems to object to the portrayal of Islam in American and world history textbooks, despite a report in 2008 from ATC that shows many of them actively glorify Islam and play down its radical tenets, while denigrating America's Judeo-Christian roots and depicting Western civilization in general as bigoted and corrupt.

In a review of ten widely used textbooks, ATC found the concepts of "jihad" and "sharia" either watered down or absent. The most pro-Islam series, *History Alive*, published by Teachers Curriculum Institute (TCI), is used or approved for use in California, Illinois, Florida, Washington state, and Texas. It defines "jihad" as "to strive," as in, "Jihad represents the human struggle to overcome difficulties and do things that are pleasing to God. Muslims strive to respond positively to personal difficulties as well as worldly challenges. For instance, they might work to become better people, reform society, or correct injustice." This book for seventh graders goes on to further define the concept of jihad: "Sometimes, however, jihad becomes a physical struggle. The Qur'an tells Muslims to fight to protect themselves from those who would do them harm or to right a terrible wrong."

ATC's report notes,

> TCI leaves "those who would do them harm" and "right a terrible wrong" to the reader's imagination. The textbook's chapter summary reads: "Muslims also have the duty of jihad, or striving to overcome challenges as they strive to please God." Since TCI describes jihad as being "the struggle against oppression," students who hear of repeated Islamic calls to jihad against Christians and Jews that include the destruction of the United States and Israel must wonder who and what is at fault.

Similar distortions of the facts about Islam occur in textbook discussions of sharia, Muslim tolerance of other religious views, and the role of women in Islam—so much so that ATC suggested that Islamic organizations might have provided some of the content that portrayed Islam in a glowing light in this academic literature for children.

But really, when you consider that some public schools now allow breaks at specific times of the school day for Muslim children to pray, you can't be all that surprised to find textbooks that promote "the religion of peace." Besides, the times they are a-changing. "Our country is transforming demographically, religiously," Edgar Hopida told the San Diego *Union-Tribune* in 2007. Hopida, a Council on American-Islamic Relations (CAIR) chapter public relations director, assumes this transformation will continue. "Our country has to now accommodate things that are not traditionally accounted for before."

Hopida said a mouthful, and if he said it in Arabic, that would be totally cool in Dearborn, Michigan, where an attempt to ban Arabic in public high school classrooms was met with outrage. (Dearborn is one of the largest Muslim cities outside the Middle East.) Attempting to respond to a study that proved bilingual programs slow assimilation into American culture and society, school officials announced a policy that teachers could only speak in languages other than English when absolutely necessary for clear communication. The response from the community? Not so fast. So of course, the school backed down. Apparently it's absolutely necessary to speak in Arabic more often than school officials figured. Besides, before long, based on all the demographic projections, Arabic will be as common on our voicemail prompts as Spanish is today.

Can You Tell Me How to Get to Shara'a Simsim?

Perhaps no entertainment property debunks the myth that media content reflects but does not shape the culture more than one iconic American institution: *Sesame Street*. Not only was this classic PBS show designed to mold young minds, it was created on the precise premise that television has the power to educate and influence children in their earliest years.

Sesame Street was created in 1969 by public TV documentary filmmaker Joan Ganz Cooney and Lloyd Morrisett, then an executive at the Carnegie Corporation with a background in early childhood education. Legend has it that Morrisett posed the question to Ganz Cooney, "Can television be used to teach young children?"

Her answer, after months of research, was a document entitled, "The Potential Uses of Television in Pre-School Education."

What resulted then was the non-profit we all knew as The Children's Television Workshop, home of Jim Henson's muppets. The organization now is called Sesame Workshop, and its mission is much greater than its original goal—to teach literacy and numeracy to America's underprivileged children. Today, *Sesame Street* is "committed to the principle that all children deserve a chance to learn and grow; to be prepared for school; to better understand the world and each other; to think, dream and discover; to reach their highest potential."

A lofty and lovely mission indeed.

Now, like most American parents, I turned on *Sesame Street* when my children were small because how else was I ever going to get to take a shower? The show was part of the rhythm of my stay-at-home life, fitting neatly between the breakfast dishes and trips to the park. Bert, Ernie, Cookie Monster, Oscar the Grouch and the *Sesame Street* grown-ups were familiar characters in our home. In fact, I once recall saying to my daughter Amy, "You're such a character," to which she responded, "No, Mom, Big Bird is a character!"

But at the risk of appearing the grouch myself, *Sesame Street* through the years became so politically correct, it seemed the focus shifted from songs and skits about letters and numbers to innumerable episodes built around diversity and multiculturalism at the expense of basic pre-school lessons. There was still a fair amount of counting, but it seemed they were mostly counting the diverse number of cultures that could be found on *Sesame Street*.

It turns out my sense that *Sesame Street* had changed direction was correct. While the show (and several others produced by Sesame Workshop) still incorporates pre-school lessons in numeracy and literacy, as well as wholesome messages about emotions and problem solving, the goal of kindergarten readiness—once the major initiative of this program—is now only one quarter of the show's agenda.

The greater goal is found in the mission statement: "to better understand the world and each other." *Sesame Street*'s commitment to multiculturalism and diversity training is found in the abundant lessons about Hispanic, African, and Asian cultures. Most notably of late, the focus has been on Palestine.

Through *The Adventures of Grover and Khokha: Sharing Arabic Culture and Arabic Language*, American children are learning about the food, transportation, clothes, recreation, and family life of Arabs. While previous generations of *Sesame Street* viewers learned Spanish words and phrases, today's pre-schoolers learn Arabic words like *fustan* (dress) and *a'ela* (family) and *ta'am* (food), not to mention Muslim traditions.

The Adventures of Grover and Khokha is only one of several initiatives intended to produce "global citizenship" in America's youngest residents. *One World, One Sky: Big Bird's Adventure* is a traveling planetarium show that "introduces children to the night sky while forging cross-cultural connections." The *Global Grover* initiative is a multi-media program for classrooms that "encourages preschoolers to understand and appreciate new people, places, and ideas." And *Panwapa* is a web-based virtual environment that "helps children gain empathy for others while encouraging a broader international perspective."

Now, here is where someone will grab a hold of this book and accuse me of all sorts of bigotry simply because I am going to question the motives of the folks at Sesame Workshop. To be clear, I am all for kids learning about various cultures! It's important to know about and appreciate the customs and lifestyles of different people around the globe.

But I question the motives of pervasive, dogmatic programming. The purpose of such initiatives—especially for very young children—is less to give them information about the world than to mold their assumptions and beliefs. Kids don't need to be taught to be curious about a cool native African costume or birthday traditions in other countries. They are natural explorers of the world around them. But through the new and improved *Sesame Street*, they're being conditioned to accept an image of themselves as "global citizens," which by definition carries a political meaning.

For example, in developing the *Panwapa* initiative, the website explains, "Sesame Workshop and the Merrill Lynch Foundation together hatched a plan to bring a global awareness curriculum to kids. They did so knowing that there was very little media available to children that would help them make sense of our ever-changing world."

Really? It seems like there's too much media! Sesame Workshop should meet the folks at the Kaiser Family Foundation, who have confirmed that American children ages eight to eighteen spend an average of seven and a half hours per day engaged with media. But wait—here's the real objective: "For example, there was no curriculum available that would teach children about the economic disparity between countries and people."

There's the code for "social and economic injustice"—which, in turn, inevitably boils down to persuading children that redistribution of wealth is the answer for the inequality in the world.

Five goals were established for the *Panwapa* program that were "identified as central to global citizenship":

- Increase children's awareness of the wider world around them

- Encourage children to appreciate similarities and value differences between themselves and others
- Instill a sense of responsibility for one's own actions
- Encourage active community participation
- Increase understanding of and response to economic disparity

A visit to Panwapa.com is like pointing and clicking through a UN children's utopia. (In case you don't know, "Panwapa" means "here on this earth" in the Tshiluba language, one of two major languages spoken in the Democratic Republic of the Congo, which, strictly speaking, is neither democratic or a republic.)

Meanwhile, Sesame Workshop also creates locally produced media in Russia, South Africa, Kosovo, Mexico, Israel, Bangladesh, France, Germany, India, Japan, Jordan, Egypt, and Palestine (where *Sesame Street* is called *Shara'a Simsim*). It's worth noting that the Sesame Workshop operates in several political hotspots. I wonder, are they as committed to diversity training in these places as they are here in the U.S.?

In Indonesia, according to SesameWorkshop.org, launching the local version of *Sesame Street*, *Jalan Sesama*, was a study in cultural cohesion, not diversity education.

> The need for cultural unity runs through [producer Ginger] Brown's mind constantly as she works on Jalan Sesama. Referring to this goal as "the touchstone for everything we're doing," she notes that the constant challenge is in identifying and nurturing a "group voice."
>
> "I think success for this show would be to further define what that [Indonesian] national voice is. If we can

do it for kids, give them a sense of what Indonesia is and what their fellow Indonesians are like, that would be great," Brown says.

Indonesian kids get to learn and celebrate Indonesian culture because it is difficult yet crucial to "create a common national voice." Given that the country is composed of some seventeen thousand islands, the show seeks to reflect the country's motto, "Bhinneka tunggal ika," or "Although in pieces, yet one."

Great motto—and so familiar! But can you imagine our American version of *Sesame Street* promoting American nationalism and our motto, *e pluribus unum*—"Out of many, one"? After years of watching the show (and believe me, I can still sing along with the kid's diversity anthem, *We All Sing With the Same Voice*) I can confidently say, they aren't promoting a quintessential American culture. Instead, the message for American children is, "Don't forget how very different we all are from one another!"

To its enormous credit, the Sesame Workshop partners with the USO as part of an initiative for military families called *Talk, Listen, Connect*. Knowing that Elmo and friends travel to U.S. bases around the world to entertain military children and that Sesame Workshop maintains a social networking web site exclusively for military families almost makes up for the fact that a great educational show for kids has been hijacked by the Left for diversity training and politically correct preschool lessons.

CHAPTER 8

CHILDREN
OF THE
NANNY STATE

Now for the bad news.

Not only is the Left succeeding in instilling anti-capitalism, moral relativism, radical environmentalism, and anti-American multiculturalism in our young people. They're also fostering a dangerous sense of entitlement and dependency in the next generation. Worst of all, they're doing it by turning the federal government into a behemoth bureaucracy financed by borrowing from the very generation they seek to indoctrinate.

Our children's attitudes and expectations about the proper role of government in their lives are measurably different from those of older generations—and entirely unlike the principles of the Founders who created the nation our children will one day inherit. While more older Americans share our Founders' vision of a limited federal government with specific, defined responsibilities, a 2010 survey commissioned by the Center for American Progress (CAP) showed younger citizens believe that the proper role of government is to solve everyday problems. (Imagine the champagne corks popping when the folks at CAP got the thumbs up from America's young adults for more government. Woot!) For example, as we'll see, an astonishing manority of Americans aged eighteen to twenty-nine believe the government should be fighting childhood obesity—not exactly the role Thomas Jefferson and James Madison foresaw for our Congress and president.

Not only do young people believe the government should be involved in our daily lives, for millions of them, government dependency already is a reality. According to the Heritage Foundation's 2010 Index of Dependence on Government, "In 2009, 64.3 million Americans depended on the government (read: their fellow citizens) for their daily housing, food, and health care." The index of dependency grew by 13.6 percent in 2009—at the same time the number of people whose tax dollars pay for entitlement programs continued to shrink. The trend has been toward increasing dependency for the entirety of our children's lives; in fact, Heritage notes, that dependency on government has increased more than fourteen times over since 1962, the first year of the forty-seven-year Index. In its summary of the 2010 report, Heritage authors William Beach and Patrick Tyrell explain why this is troubling:

> It is the conjunction of these two trends—higher spending on dependence-creating programs and an ever-shrinking number of taxpayers who pay for these programs—that worries those interested in the fate of the American form of government. Americans have always expressed concern about becoming dependent on

government, even while understanding that life's challenges cause most people, at one time or another, to
depend on aid from someone else. Americans' concern
stems partly from deeply held views that life's blessings
are more readily obtained by independent people and
that growing dependence on government erodes the
spirit of self-reliance and self-improvement.

Yet government intrusion is now so commonplace that young Americans don't think of it as intrusion at all. Heck, President Obama is
as familiar to them as the principal of their school.

Principal Obama Rings the Bell

In 2009, Barack Obama took to the Internet via the White House
website to deliver an unprecedented first-day-of-school address to
millions of students in pre-school through twelfth grade. The speech
was announced to school principals across the country in a letter
Secretary of Education Arne Duncan sent to roughly fourteen thousand school districts and "as many of the 100,000+ public and private schools as we could reach," according to the Department of
Education (ED) website. (FAQs on the site indicate the speech was
"not mandatory," which seems to suggest someone at ED thought
they could make it so.) Billed as an inspirational message on the
importance of staying in school, the speech created a stir days
beforehand thanks to the companion materials released by ED.
These materials, meant as lesson plans to expand upon Obama's
themes, struck a decidedly political tone that didn't escape the notice
of parents and the general public. Included on the "Menu of Classroom Activities" for pre-K to sixth graders was one the White House
later admitted was "inartfully" phrased, suggesting that students

"Write letters to themselves about what they can do to help the president."

After a nationwide uproar about the use of classrooms as partisan political Petri dishes, the activity for students was changed to "Write letters to themselves about how they can achieve their short-term and long-term educational goals." Setting aside the snooze-worthy nature of such a task for pre-K through sixth graders, you have to wonder about the utility of this exercise, if not to connect America's children to their "Dear Leader" by celebrating his unprecedented appearance in their classrooms.

Classroom materials for students in grades seven through twelve focus more overtly on the students' connection to Obama. These older kids' teachers were encouraged to utilize quotes from Obama's speeches on education so that the students could understand the president's message. Questions for discussion included, "How will President Obama inspire us? How will he challenge us? And why did he want to speak to us today?"

Presumably, "to indoctrinate us" was not one of the answers sought by ED.

Yet the bungled attempt to provide pro-Obama lesson plans deflected attention from the deeper issue, namely, the underlying message contained in the president's speech to America's children. On the surface, the speech read like a parental lecture. Or maybe one from a well-meaning but boring uncle. President Obama's supporters portrayed it as a pep rally on the importance of hard work as a key ingredient to school success—a worthy message with which no one could find fault.

But for conservatives, the speech struck a disturbing chord. The tenor of Obama's talk to America's youth was both overly personal and intrusively instructive. The president seemed to assume a role in the lives of his audience that simply is not his to claim. After sharing tales of his own early education in Indonesia—which he claimed included doses of homeschooling from his mother in the wee hours to augment his lessons (some call this "tutoring")—Obama articulated his mission: "I'm here today because I want to talk with you about your education and what's expected of all of you in this new school year...."

Obama wove himself seamlessly into the lives of America's children by implying that he has an appropriate role to play in setting expectations for their school performance and behavior.

He doesn't. That is, unless we're a socialist country, in which case the government reserves for itself the proper education and formation of its children.

Otherwise, in a free society, setting expectations for kids' lives is the job of parents, who may choose public schools among a variety of educational options. Only their parents and the teachers and school administrators that parents choose to entrust with their education—not the chief executive of our federal government—should be communicating expectations for children for the coming school year.

This mission creep has been inevitable ever since the federal government began involving itself in matters of education. Public schools are meant to be state and local entities. But even though the vast majority of their funding is from state and local taxes, our public schools have increasingly become an arm of the federal bureaucracy—one that can be mobilized by the Secretary of Education for any purpose he and the president deem appropriate. (In this case, wasting a solid half hour of the first day of school.)

Having asserted, socialist-style, a position of direct authority in children's lives, Obama assured them that he is an actor on the educational stage:

Now, your families, your teachers, and I are doing everything we can to make sure you have the education you
need.... *I'm working hard to fix up your classrooms and
get you the books and the equipment and the computers
you need to learn.* [emphasis added]

Children wouldn't understand that when the president says, "I'm
working hard," he was referring to his alliance with the NEA to shake
down taxpayers for more than just the measly 10 percent of local
school funding that comes from the federal budget. Perhaps children
assumed President Obama was sitting in the Oval Office, choosing
textbooks and computers, and also phoning the school to see that
the janitors were coming in to sweep the classrooms. His personal
testimony to his hard work on their behalf was meant to assure millions of school kids that he, Barack Obama, is intimately and appropriately involved in their educations, and thus, their daily lives.

The most insidious socialist message contained in the speech
was likely intended to be inspirational. But in fact the president
offered his young audience a list of statist life goals:

What you make of your education will decide nothing less
than the future of this country.... You'll need the knowledge and problem-solving skills you learn in science and
math to cure diseases like cancer and AIDS, and to
develop new energy technologies and protect our environment. You'll need the insights and critical thinking
skills you gain in history and social studies to fight poverty and homelessness, crime and discrimination, and
make our nation more fair and more free. You'll need
the creativity and ingenuity you develop in all your
classes to build new companies that will create new jobs

and boost our economy. *We need every single one of you to develop your talents, skills and intellect so you can help solve our most difficult problems. If you don't do that—if you quit on school—you're not just quitting on yourself, you're quitting on your country.* [emphasis added]

There's the bottom line. The government will educate you, he says, and then your obligation is to serve the government's goals, not your own. You have to "develop your talents, skills and intellect" *not* to one day realize your dreams or support your family, but to "solve our most difficult problems."

Suburban liberals—the soccer parents who wear athletic socks with their Birkenstocks and already have "Obama '12" stickers on the bumpers of their Saabs—will accuse me of over-analyzing this speech. They'll say I'm looking for reasons to dislike the president, for who could object to a politically benign and personally motivating message such as the one he delivered on the opening day of the 2009 school year?

They may agree with me that it's a message that would better be delivered by mom and dad over a family meal at the end of the day. But what about all those poor kids who don't have family meals, or even a mom and dad to eat with? They need to be pushed to work hard as well.

I must be prejudiced against all the poor, single-parented children in America, especially the ones without a dad at home to give a tough-love, work-hard message on the first day of the new school year. Isn't it the role of our wise and caring president—himself a model father—to step in and do what too many fathers don't do?

There it is: a little bit of "compassion" plus the hint of an accusation of racism, and you've justified allowing the federal government to sweep in to do what individuals ought rightly to do.

When the government does the job of a parent, that's socialism.

Midway through the 2009-2010 school year, apropos of nothing, the president weighed in with some tough love on media consumption. In the spirit of parent-teacher conferences (or would this be parent-president conferences?), Obama advised America's mothers and fathers to limit children's TV time to weekends only. Our "Dear Leader" strikes again.

Not content to launch the academic year in the fall or to dispense mid-year instructions on media consumption for parents and children, Obama in the spring also shared his vision of statism with graduating seniors.

Through its Race to the Top Commencement Challenge, the Obama administration selected Kalamazoo Central High School in Kalamazoo, Michigan, as the site of the Principal-In-Chief's closing message for the 2010 school year. (Unfortunately, the White House's selection committee didn't anticipate that Obama's speech would cause one graduate, sitting just over the president's shoulder, to doze on camera during the address. Oops.)

Of course, fairness required that the president come up with a way to influence the rest of the nation's three-million-odd high school grads as well. This imperative prompted a *Parade* magazine piece called "A Message to the Class of 2010," which began, "Since I couldn't be at every high school and college commencement this year, I wanted to send a message to all of the graduates in this country who are about to embark on the next chapter of your young and promising lives."

Am I the only one who thinks he meant that? Seriously. He really would have spoken at every commencement if he could have.

Oddly enough, in the first several paragraphs of his message, Obama suggested that those young lives are not remotely promising. If the president meant to communicate optimism for the future, one questions this opener:

"There are generations of Americans who came of age during periods of peace and prosperity. When they graduated from high school or college, they entered a world of comfort and stability where little was required of them beyond their obligations to themselves and their families. That is not the world you are about to inherit."

Against this cheerless backdrop, Obama exhorted America's young adults to have hope. Not that things will get better, but—wait for the socialist undertone—that the country can be "changed": "While America's destiny is never certain, our ability to shape it always is. Ours is a history of renewal and reinvention, where each generation finds a way to adapt, thrive, and push the nation forward with energy, ingenuity, and optimism."

Most troubling was the flat-out demonizing of capitalism and personal ambition found in the president's call to "public service."

> While government plays a role in making a more prosperous and secure future possible for America, the final outcome ultimately depends on you and the choices you make from here on out. *Of course, each of you has the right to take your diploma and seek the quickest path to the biggest paycheck or the highest title possible. But remember: you can choose to broaden your concerns to include your fellow citizens and country instead.* By tying your ambitions to America's, you'll hitch your wagon to a cause larger than yourself. [emphasis added]

Obama is telling our nation's new graduates they can either go looking for a fat paycheck or they can serve their fellow citizens. They can't do both. But wait a minute. If everyone goes into "public service," who will pay the taxes for all the entitlement programs? Oh, never mind.

Whenever Obama speaks directly to students, the intention is clear: to instill an expectation that he and the federal government play a personal role in their daily lives, and to undermine any personal goals or aspirations they may hold in their hearts (how greedy!). Instead, he recommends as virtuous only those pursuits that fall under his (very broad) definition of public service.

Mama Obama and the Food Police

No one is for obesity. So obesity provides the perfect opportunity for the government to manipulate and control our behavior under the guise of doing what is best for us. For our children's generation, government involvement in the issue of food consumption, obesity, and health will simply be a given. But the good news is that's apparently what our young people want and expect. (And by the good news, I mean the alarming trend.)

According to a March 2011 poll from the Pew Research Center, more than half of Americans—57 percent—believe the government should play a role in fighting the childhood obesity epidemic. But here's the really disheartening stat: among eighteen- to twenty-nine-year-olds, that figure is 69 percent. The *vast majority* of young adults believe the federal government of the United States of America should play a "significant role."

But wait. Is there a childhood obesity epidemic?

There must be. The White House has decreed it so.

Childhood obesity is certainly a bad thing. Obese kids are at increased risk of developing a long list of medical maladies, and most notably, of maintaining an unhealthy weight throughout adulthood. And over 19 percent of children between the ages of six and eleven, and 18 percent of twelve- to nineteen-year-olds are now clinically obese. According to one report from the Centers for Disease Control (CDC), obesity in children has more than tripled in the past thirty years.

Or maybe not. A March 2011 *New England Journal of Medicine* article questions the assumptions of the CDC's statistical analyses, saying, "Results from the CDC's 2007–2008 National Health and Nutrition Examination Survey (NHANES) suggest that the prevalence of obesity among women (35.5%) and children 2 to 19 years of age (16.9%) has remained stable over the past 10 years and that the prevalence among men (32.2%) has not changed significantly since 2003. These conflicting reports have led to confusion regarding the prevalence of, and secular trends in, obesity in the United States."

Several credible social scientists have boldly asserted that obesity simply isn't as big a deal as the government is making it out to be. Appearing in February 2010 on Freakonomics Radio with *Freakonomics* authors Stephen Dubner and Steven Levitt, two experts said there's politics lurking in the underbelly of obesity (sorry, couldn't resist).

Eric Oliver, professor of sociology at the University of Chicago and author of *Fat Politics: The Real Story Behind America's Obesity Epidemic*, explained that the problem began when CDC released some research in a 2004 edition of the *Journal of the American Medical Association* (JAMA) that said obesity was killing four hundred thousand Americans a year.

That's as many people as live in Cleveland, Ohio, dying every year from obesity. Did the mainstream media question this study? Heck no. Headlines above the fold.

Shortly after the JAMA article, a different division of the CDC, using more current data and more accurate computations, claimed the number was more like twenty thousand people per year—and that there were just as many people dying from being underweight as from being overweight.

Brian Wansink, a researcher at Cornell University, a former nutrition official at the Department of Agriculture, and author of the bestselling book *Mindless Eating: Why We Eat More Than We Think*, also appeared on the Freakonomics radio show and said, "There's a tremendous number of people who profit by hyping obesity. I don't think it's the epidemic that a lot of people paint it as, but here's who profits... there's a huge number of academics who benefit by doing this, because there is so much money in grants, whether it be the NIH grant, or CDC or whatever, that is out there, if academics can make the case that this is a huge, fat world that's just going to heck—they benefit. I'm not saying there isn't a problem. But I'm saying it gets really blown out of proportion because there are a lot of people who are motivated to do so."

Radical Leftists are among the most motivated because a major health crisis is the perfect excuse to insert the government into people's everyday lives. Especially the fat ones. And as we all know, once a crisis has been firmly established in the media, there's no stopping the expansion of government.

Ergo, the childhood obesity train has pulled out of the station and is rolling toward a utopian future where Michelle Obama will eradicate childhood chub in one generation.

The Obama White House, which in theory was going to be science-driven, is actually crisis-driven, and this issue represents a terrific emergency. The kind of crisis this administration will not let go to waste. "The childhood obesity epidemic in America is a national health crisis," says the White House's Task Force on Childhood Obesity, of which Michelle Obama is the chair. Citing that claim that one in three American children is overweight or obese, the First Lady has targeted this issue as one of her areas of concentration.

And talk about an opportunity! The childhood obesity crisis, implicating as it does our educational potential, our military readiness, and our economic competitiveness, offers unlimited avenues into the everyday lives of American citizens. "We have a roadmap for implementing our plan across our government and across the country," Mrs. Obama said when the report was released.

How will she accomplish this? The public relations arm of the program—the only task that is remotely appropriate for a First Lady—is her "Let's Move" campaign, for which she travels the nation encouraging kids to get more exercise and eat more leafy green veggies. There is not a person in America who could argue against the merits of this effort. I certainly won't. Have at it, Mrs. O.

But of course, there's a whole lot more to the Obama administration's anti-obesity agenda than getting the superstar Beyoncé Knowles to rewrite the lyrics to her racy song "Get Me Bodied" so it's appropriate for a middle school flash mob. (That happened.)

No, as per usual, the devil is in the details. The report from the Task Force included *seventy* specific recommendations, summarized thusly in a White House press release:

- Getting children a healthy start on life, with good prenatal care for their parents; support for breastfeeding; adherence to limits on "screen time"; and quality child care settings with nutritious food and ample opportunity for young children to be physically active.
- Empowering parents and caregivers with simpler, more actionable messages about nutritional choices based on the latest Dietary Guidelines for Americans; improved labels on food and menus that provide clear information to help parents make healthy choices for children; reduced marketing of unhealthy products to children; and improved health care services, including BMI measurement for all children.

- Providing healthy food in schools, through improvements in federally supported school lunches and breakfasts; upgrading the nutritional quality of other foods sold in schools; and improving nutrition education and the overall health of the school environment.
- Improving access to healthy, affordable food, by eliminating "food deserts" in urban and rural America; lowering the relative prices of healthier foods; developing or reformulating food products to be healthier; and reducing the incidence of hunger, which has been linked to obesity.
- Getting children more physically active, through quality physical education, recess, and other opportunities in and after school; addressing aspects of the "built environment" that make it difficult for children to walk or bike safely in their communities; and improving access to safe parks, playgrounds, and indoor and outdoor recreational facilities.

It cannot be said often enough that this menu of Nanny State solutions would insert the federal government into virtually every aspect of our lives.

On Freakonomics Radio, Wansink said, "There's a couple of really critical things that are missing from the 'Let's Move' policy. It's been tried fifteen different times and it's never been effective." But what does he know? He only worked as a government nutritionist and helped devise the food pyramid.

Again I have to say, no one is for obesity. I am not for obesity. You are not for obesity. Obese people struggling with the ramifications of obesity are not for obesity. Nonetheless, obesity is a health problem for individuals and families to tackle. Because losing our liberty in the name of a healthier population is going to cause us more regret than a snack of Krispy Kremes and Mountain Dew.

One might wonder why the government believes it can solve the childhood obesity problem when its own massive National School Lunch Program—feeding children free (or at least subsidized) lunches since 1946—may in fact be one of the root causes of the problem. Inconveniently, at around the same time Michelle Obama was introducing the "Let's Move" logo, researchers at the University of Michigan Cardiovascular Center released a paper at the American College of Cardiology's fifty-ninth annual scientific session indicating that children who consume school lunches are more likely to be overweight or obese than those who bring lunches from home.

The University of Michigan also noted, "Recent data show that while an estimated 30.6 million U.S. students consume school lunches, only 6 percent of school lunch programs meet the requirements established by the School Meals Initiative for Healthy Children."

You'd think, then, that schools would encourage parents to pack lunches at home, right? In theory, the more kids eat homemade lunches, the better their nutritional intake.

Not in the wacky world we live in. Students at Little Village Academy, within the Chicago Public School system, are not permitted to bring a lunch from home. Little Village banned sack lunches six years ago in a supposed effort to improve the nutritional quality of the food its students consume.

According to a *Chicago Tribune* report, Chicago Public Schools (CPS) permits its principals to use their discretion to decide if their student population needs stringent rules about food choices. Apparently several CPS schools have banned sack lunches, while others permit them but confiscate certain foods that administrators deem unhealthy (think Doritos, soda, candy).

Problem: the Little Village students hate much of the school's cafeteria food. Lunches are routinely thrown away uneaten, leaving kids hungry until they get home at the end of the day. Bigger problem: it's not the role of a public school principal to decree what her students may and may not eat.

I'm not arguing against the merits of a healthier school lunch. As the mother of four children, I've already packed thousands of lunches for the very purpose of assuring the nutritional value of my kids' midday meal, and I have about nine hundred to go, give or take. But unfortunately, Little Village parents who want to pack lunches that are even healthier than those prepared in the school cafeteria are unable to do so. (The school makes exceptions only for children with allergies or special dietary needs.) The kids profiled in the *Chicago Tribune* story said they'd rather bring a sandwich and a banana from home than eat the glop that passes for "healthy" enchiladas on their lunch trays.

At the heart of the anti-obesity agenda is the underlying belief that some parents are simply incapable of making wise decisions on behalf of their own children—even about what to feed them for lunch.

And okay, some are incapable. Or at least they don't seem to understand why it's a bad idea to send a six-year-old to school with a can of soda and bag of Doritos. But if we can't trust people to pack their own children's lunch—even if they won't always handle it perfectly—then what responsibility can we trust them with? Assuming for the sake of argument that the folks at Little Village Academy and other schools are simply responding to the lack of solid parenting they see exhibited as junk food in sack lunches, the fact remains: the road to tyranny is paved with good intentions.

The folks who advocate such mandated programs always make what sounds like an irrefutable argument: the school (read: government) must step in for our children's health and wellness.

And voilà! The Healthy, Hunger-Free Kids Act of 2010, which, based on past efforts of our federal government, will neither assure children's health nor alleviate their hunger. But it will feed the growth of the Nanny State.

Only the Government Can Call You Fat

Based on the flawed reasoning that parents are unable to monitor and promote the good health of their own children, schools across the nation now are requiring Body Mass Index analyses for students. BMI, a formula based on height and weight, is notoriously unreliable for kids because their bodies are growing quickly. In children, BMI isn't necessarily a useful indicator of fitness. (It's not even very useful in adults since muscle weighs more than fat. Professional athletes often are rated overweight based on this rough-and-ready body-fat test.)

No matter. In 2010, nine-year-old Shelby Sumner underwent a BMI analysis at her school in Medway, Massachusetts. Shelby is a gymnast and athlete, and by all accounts (or at least as evidenced in the MyFoxBoston.com news reel), she's as fit as a fiddle. But school officials calculated the BMI of this ninety-pound, four-foot-nine child in the "overweight" range.

Her mother, Lori-Ann Sumner, was understandably upset, but also concerned about the impact the "fat letters" would have on other, more sensitive children. Turns out this is a valid concern.

In Buckeye, Arizona, the mother of a junior high student cried foul when her eleven-year-old daughter was given a BMI report indicating she is obese. The letter wasn't mailed to the home or even handed to the student in an envelope, but stapled to the BMI report and given to the student to take home. Already struggling with self-esteem and body-image concerns, the girl was humiliated because her peers knew what the letter said.

Her mother, Deborah Delabruere, took to the media to lambast the school district for invading her daughter's privacy and for causing her emotional harm. The response from the school? A report from MyFoxPhoenix.com says, "The school district's superintendent, Al Steen, says weight is a sensitive issue but does not admit any wrongdoing. 'It's always easy to hindsight and second guess, but we can't be concerned about that. But what I will say is that we're always concerned about the wellness of our children,' he says."

Wow. Someone sign this guy up for the next White House bullying summit. He gets it.

According to the website of the Center for Consumer Freedom, school-based harassment (excuse me, intervention in the best interests of the children) of overweight students has failed in the past:

> Incredibly, this isn't the first time this has been tried. Arkansas made the same mistake by mandating that schools issue fat report cards back in 2003. The completely predictable result was that 13 percent of parents said their kids had been teased at school because of the program while the state reported absolutely no drop in childhood obesity.

Beyond the schools, government regulation is expanding the role of radical Leftists acting as "food police" in our lives. Whether it's banning Happy Meals in San Francisco or soda and salt in New York, trans fat limits for restaurants or zoning laws meant to eradicate fast food chains, the war on unhealthy food is really a war on personal freedom. Declaring that some foods are "Foods of Minimal Nutritional Value" (FMNV) means schools can regulate birthday treats and the government can regulate advertising and commerce—all in the name of protecting our health.

Thanks to the radical Left, our children may grow up to be the fittest generation of government serfs that ever lived. Now that's something to celebrate. Carrot juice for everyone!

PART THREE:

WINNING THE HEARTS AND MINDS OF OUR CHILDREN

CHAPTER 9

RESTORING AMERICA IN THE NEXT GENERATION

Did I mention the North Carolina second grader whose public school teacher coached her to lobby her daddy, a state legislator, against cuts to the state's education budget?

Did I tell you about the proposal under consideration by the Maine Civil Rights commission to gender-neutralize its education system—including a ban on gender-based bathrooms in elementary schools?

Did I mention Massachusetts' Concord-Carlisle High School's performance, over parental objections, of the Tony-award-winning play *Falsettos*, the tale of a bisexual father torn between his family and his gay lover?

Come to think of it, I don't think I mentioned the eight-year-old Massachusetts boy who was sent home from school and ordered to undergo a psychiatric evaluation for sketching a stick figure of Jesus hanging on a cross. That's the case in which a father was told his son had created a "violent drawing" and could not return to school until he had undergone testing at the parent's expense. The psychologist determined there was nothing wrong with the child.

And how could I have forgotten to include the Provincetown, Massachusetts, School Board's decision to extend its free condom program to its elementary school, which serves students in kindergarten through sixth grade. (The policy requires that a student seeking a condom first receive counseling, including how to wear a condom, and information on abstinence. The policy does not include notifying parents of the child's request.)

I feel like I may have cheated you out of some truly compelling examples of Leftist radicalism in the lives of our children.

Of course, a book like this can be only a snapshot of the social and political landscape that is influencing our nation's children and molding their beliefs and expectations. My difficulty in researching and writing about the Kool-Aid culture in which we live is that each new day offers up more preposterous and alarming examples of Leftism in action.

Leftists consider these episodes victories. The rest of us shake our heads and wonder how such things are happening in the United States of America. Those of us who are trying to instill in our children the civic virtues that have heretofore defined our nation may wonder if we're engaged in a hopeless effort after all.

But if I truly believed our efforts were pointless, mine would be simply another voice in the cacophony of complaints about America. The last thing our country needs is another hand-wringing whiner.

My goal has been to convince you that Leftists in positions of power and influence over our children are seriously undermining the values and virtues essential to our national character and to American citizenship. But more than that, my aim is to motivate you to respond personally, publicly, and politically to this fundamental threat to our unique form of government and our extraordinary way of life.

It's not enough to simply shrug our shoulders in resignation. To capitulate to the Left's hijacking of America's next generation is to betray the legacy of our Founders—not to mention our children. They deserve the right as citizens to enjoy the blessings of liberty that generations of Americans have preserved for them.

It is clear that the Left is winning the battle of ideas with America's young people, and doing so with some decidedly mediocre political dogma. If our children are both demonstrably uneducated and measurably indoctrinated, and if we're fully aware that these things are true, we can't just stand around clucking and griping about all that is wrong. We need to offer more of what is right.

If we want our children to experience the liberty and opportunity uniquely available to us as American citizens, we need to raise a new generation of leaders who will shore up the republican form of government handed down to us by our Founders. We need to counter the Left's messages about dependency and entitlement with a vision of patriotic citizenship to which our youth can aspire.

That's a lofty ideal. And let's face it, we already have our hands full with the demands of working, caring for children or elderly relatives (or both), maintaining our homes, participating in church and community groups, and simply living from day to day. Still, those of us with the opportunity to inspire and educate young people, through whatever roles we play in their lives, must accept responsibility for the most important contribution any adult can make to his or her society—the caliber of citizens being raised for the future.

Protecting the Rights of Parents

It should go without saying that in the United States of America, parents enjoy the fundamental right to direct their children's upbringing and care, manage decisions about their education and health, and otherwise safeguard and promote their emotional, physical, intellectual, spiritual, and moral development.

But if we've learned anything in the preceding chapters of this book, it's that nothing goes without saying.

At the same time that the radical Left has undermined the very structure of the family in our nation by altering the definition of the bonds of family, our Leftist federal judiciary has begun to weaken the authority of parents to exercise their God-given rights to raise their children.

Historically, the courts upheld parents' rights. In more than a dozen cases going as far back as 1923, courts recognized and honored the unique role of parents in society. But we've come a long way since 1944, when the decision in the case of *Prince v. Commonwealth of Massachusetts*, 321 U.S. 158, included this reassurance:

> It is cardinal with us that the custody, care and nurture of the child reside first in the parents, whose primary function and freedom include preparation for obligations the state can neither supply nor hinder.... It is in recognition of this that these decisions have respected the private realm of family life which the state cannot enter.

More recent cases indicate the Left's ever-growing influence. For example, lower courts in West Virginia assigned full custody to a child's babysitters on the premise that they were "psychological parents" to the girl. Initially, the child's mother was only permitted visitation with her daughter four times a week at a McDonald's. The mother had never been accused of abuse or found to be unfit, yet the appeals court still required that she share custody with the babysitters. Only after the case made its way to the West Virginia Supreme Court was full custody of the child awarded to her mother, with admonishment from the highest court that parenting is "the paramount right in the world." *In Re: Visitation and Custody of Senturi N.S.V.,* 221 W.Va. 159, 652 S.E. 2d 490 (2007).

Yet this paramount right has been under attack by the Left for at least a generation. In a landmark case in Washington State in the early 1980s, the parents of thirteen-year-old Sheila Marie Sumey became concerned that she was involved in drugs and engaging in inappropriate sexual behavior, so they grounded her. But Sheila complained to a school counselor who informed her that she could be emancipated from her parents if she was substantially in conflict with them. Instructed to contact Child Protective Services, Sheila got herself removed from her parents' home and put into foster care. Her parents sought her return, but despite the fact that a judge found their rules and discipline were entirely reasonable, they lost. *In Re: Sumey,* 94 Wn. 2d 757, 621 P. 2d 108 (1980).

It's hard to imagine anything more heartbreaking than attempting to do what you believe is best for your child, only to be confounded in fulfilling your responsibility by intrusive statists who believe they know better than parents. This strategy on the part of the Left reveals their agenda. The most heinous examples are abortion laws that protect the privacy of minor girls in obtaining "reproductive health services" from their parents' involvement in the most life-altering decisions. As is often noted, a teenager can't get so much as an aspirin at a school clinic without written permission from her parents, but in many states she can have traumatic, psychologically damaging, irreparable surgery in the form of an abortion—and mom and dad have no right to know.

But the core principle behind rules barring parental notification of abortion is the same principle behind the ban against homemade school lunches. It's the notion that the state's ideas about what constitutes children's "best interest" trump those of their parents.

Legal scholars affiliated with the organization Parentalrights.org warn that the trend toward state control over parental decision-making is only gaining ground. Without a stated provision in the federal Constitution to protect the supremacy of parents in the upbringing of their children, courts will continue to erode this fundamental, God-given role.

More alarming still, the radical Left's infatuation with globalism will further erode parents' rights, thanks to an international treaty that is meant to put all the world's children under the care and keeping of the state.

Now, if you're a parent, you're probably too busy doing the day-to-day work of raising your children to worry about an international treaty that could actually undermine your authority over them. But if you've ever insisted that your teenager drag himself out of bed on a Sunday morning to attend church with the family, or required him to find a part-time job to pay for the increase in your car insurance, or—heaven forbid—if you've ever spanked a young child for an act of willful disobedience, then you should know, there are powerful folks who'd like to override your parental judgment.

Folks like President Obama, in fact.

The issue of parental rights is at the heart of the ongoing debate over the failure of the United States to ratify the United Nation's Convention on the Rights of the Child (CRC). President Obama thinks it's a travesty that the U.S. and Somalia—a country not known as a beacon of human rights—are the only two nations that haven't ratified this treaty.

Up to now, it's been a worried American homeschooling community that most vocally opposes the CRC. That's because the treaty clearly places responsibility for the education of children in the hands of the federal government. Such a mandate would certainly threaten the freedom of states to allow, and of parents to choose, homeschooling as an option to educate their children.

But it's not just homeschooling parents who ought to be nervous about the CRC. We all should be. The language of the treaty—which would supersede all American law other than the Constitution—radically changes the authority structure between parents, children, and the state. In short, in line after line, it applies the standard of "the best interests of the child" to determine what's permissible and what isn't.

For example, the treaty creates "the right of the child to freedom of thought, conscience and religion." So if your child doesn't want to go to a religious school, the law would favor his preference, not your desire to instill your faith.

It prohibits "arbitrary or unlawful interference with his or her privacy," which means you'd better not snoop in your son's pockets while sorting the laundry. Warrantless search and seizure of his blue jeans could literally be illegal, and too bad if you find something to set off your parental alarm.

The CRC also affirms the UN's goal of eliminating small firearms and imposing global gun control, and keeping arms from children at all times. So much for hunter safety class when you turn twelve, son.

In fact, in Scotland, a CRC nation, a pamphlet for children explaining how they are helped by the treaty says, "In Scotland, the law recognises that your parents should normally be the people who care for you, if it's the best thing for you."

That's very different from a provision that might say, "You have the right to the protection and care of your parents and can only be removed from your family if you are the victim of abuse or neglect." The reason it doesn't read this way is because that's not what the CRC intends.

And who decides what's "the best thing"? Take a guess.

It makes sense that the U.S. stands nearly alone in refusing to ratify this treaty, since we live in the safest, most prosperous, most desirable country in which to be a child.

The CRC might make sense in places where girls can be sold into marriage at age ten, or where children are routinely victims of the sex trade, or of child labor abuse.

But in the U.S., the only logical reason to sign the CRC is to expand the role of the federal government into the daily lives and decisions of American parents and families.

Avoiding ratification of the CRC is an important step to protect the rights of America's parents, but passage of a Parent's Rights Amendment to the Federal Constitution would assure that the proper authority and autonomy of parents to direct and support their children is upheld. Visit Parentalrights.org and learn more.

Recalibrating Our Moral Compass

Despite the chasm of time and technology that separates us from our Founders, they actually offered amazing insight into the issues that face modern-day American families. In his farewell address to the nation in 1796, President George Washington reminded his fellow citizens present and future, "Of all the dispositions and habits which lead to political prosperity, religion and morality are indispensable supports."

This timeless statement must direct our response to the radical Left's assault on our families and our faith.

The current generation of young Americans is inarguably in dire need of a recalibrated moral compass. A longitudinal study of teen ethics conducted biennially by the Josephson Institute of Ethics (forty thousand teens were surveyed in 2010) finds "entrenched" habits of immoral, unethical, and dishonest conduct. The Josephson Institute's press release explained,

> While 89 percent of students believe that being a good person is more important than being rich, almost one in three boys and one in four girls admitted stealing from a store within the past year. Moreover, 21 percent admitted they stole something from a parent or other relative, and 18 percent admitted stealing from a friend.
>
> On lying, more than two in five said they sometimes lie to save money (48 percent of males and 35 percent of females). While 92 percent of students believe their parents want them to do the right thing, more than eight in ten confessed they lied to a parent about something significant.
>
> Rampant cheating in school continues. A majority of students (59 percent) admitted cheating on a test during the last year, with 34 percent doing it more than two times. One in three admitted they used the Internet to plagiarize an assignment.
>
> "As bad as these numbers are, they appear to be understated," said Michael Josephson, president of the Institute and a national leader in ethics training. "More than one in four students confessed they lied on at least one or two survey questions, which is typically an attempt to conceal misconduct."

Alarmingly, fully 92 percent of students surveyed said they were satisfied with their ethics and character, despite admitting to habitually unethical practices.

How did we manage to get to a point where our children seem to make no connection between their behavior and the character it reflects?

Undeniably, public figures of all political stripes have helped to foster the notion that actions and authentic character are unrelated. The image of a politician crying in humiliation after his debauched conduct is revealed, only to proclaim he is not resigning from office because his actions don't reflect on his ability to do his job, is now a cliché. (Except Anthony Weiner. He's a cartoon.)

But the radical Left's influence on educational theory and parenting philosophy are more to blame. Thanks to the so-called self-esteem movement in schools, our children have learned that everyone is always good, even when they make mistakes and that whatever consequences they might suffer for their actions never speak to the inherent character within a child's heart.

Leftist parenting experts have taught baby boomer moms and dads never to spank, and certainly never to label our children as "good" or "bad" boys and girls, as this will damage their tiny psyches. Now an entire generation thinks lying to their parents or cheating on tests are only poor choices that mean nothing about the goodness of their character.

But as Josephson's research has affirmed time and again, our neglect of our children's moral development *is* sadly and crucially evident in our American character. And it is most certainly evident in the cruelty our children exert and experience through bullying.

The bullying problem—oh sorry, epidemic—in America also reflects the moral vacuum in which our children are being raised, and as we've seen, it is being used to promote the gay political agenda. The real cause of bullying is not intolerance for people who are different. It is a lack of conscience and character in the hearts and souls of our children.

The case of Rutgers University freshman Tyler Clementi illustrates perfectly both the root cause of bullying and the Left's shameless exploitation of this issue. In October 2010, you may recall Tyler was unknowingly videoed while in the privacy of his dorm room by two fellow students who authorities say were his roommate, Dharun Ravi, and another student, Molly Wei. Knowing Tyler would be engaged in a gay sexual encounter, Ravi set up a camera in the room so that he and Wei could stream the video live online, police said.

Upon learning of his mistreatment, young Tyler sought redress through university housing authorities, but apparently he was unable to endure the public humiliation to which he had been subjected. His Facebook status, "Jumping off the gw bridge sorry," conveyed in its brevity his helpless desperation.

Tyler's tragic suicide left a heartbroken family and a bewildered community that struggled to understand why a shy, unassuming, and accomplished person was the target of such a despicable invasion of privacy.

The quick and politically expedient answer is that he was gay. Public outcry from every corner—including Secretary of Education Arne Duncan and entertainer Ellen DeGeneres—focused on Tyler Clementi's sexuality as the reason he was targeted. What was needed, they said, was diversity training so that kids would become more empathetic to people who are different.

But the theory—that kids will cease to belittle students for nonconforming sexuality because of early sensitivity training—will only put more teens and young adults at risk of bullying, depression, and suicide. Kids don't need to be taught about sexual preference. They need to be taught right from wrong.

I don't believe Tyler's roommate and another friend invaded his privacy to stream his sexual encounter online because he was gay. Early news reports included quotations—from people who knew both students—suggesting that they had histories of accepting gay friends and were more amused than appalled by Tyler's sexuality.

They did it because they have no conscience.

The question we should be asking in the aftermath of this tragedy and countless other bullying episodes isn't, "How can we protect gay students?" It's, "What kind of person would do such a thing to another human being?"

This story was not about homosexuality. It was about kids who were never taught to conform to a societal standard of morality, decency, and civility that would result in genuine respect for others. And it's about what happens when there is no behavioral code in which the bullying of another person is always unthinkable.

If we continue to buy into the knee-jerk Leftist reaction that what's needed is more sexual education and greater advocacy of the gay agenda, we're selling short all kids—gay and straight. What they need instead is character education.

Our children are lacking the one thing that sets them toward true north in moral decision-making: a conscience. Visit CharacterCounts. org and learn more.

Renewing Our Children's Innocence

In January 2010, when the Kaiser Family Foundation released its study, "Generation M2: Media in the Lives of 8-18 Year Olds," headlines registered shock and outrage. "Researchers shocked at kids' online time," said one. "U.S. kids using media almost 8 hours a day," another screamed. "New media use by children up by hours per week," another story warned.

Essentially, the news coverage at the unveiling of the updated research on children, teens, and the media focused on the sheer quantity of media consumed by America's youths. This was newsworthy, to be sure. The very idea that children and teens are physically able to absorb more than fifty-three hours per week of media content—or 7:38 per day—astonished even the researchers who had believed that the previous average of 6:21 per day calculated in 2004 represented a maximum.

Even more mind-boggling, thanks to multitasking (using more than one kind of media at a time), children and teens "actually manage to pack a total of 10 hours and 45 minutes (10:45) worth of media content into those 7½ hours," the KFF study said. A note to the already astonished: the study didn't include the time kids spend texting via cell phones. Add another hour and a half per day.

As the mother of four, I wondered at the time if the folks who were surprised by this research have children. It strikes me that only the childless would be shocked by the results. The rest of us spend much of our time saying things like, "Turn off the computer and go to bed." Those who wonder how it's possible that a child can rack up more time using electronic media than most people spend earning a living are perhaps unaware that over 70 percent of American children have television sets in their bedrooms. Most kids also personally own computers, gaming systems, and, increasingly, mobile devices that provide full access to the Internet. Notably, most children have no rules about when and how they may use their electronics.

According to the study, "Only about three in ten young people say they have rules about how much time they can spend watching TV (28%) or playing video games (30%), and 36% say the same about using the computer. But when parents *do* set limits, children spend less time with media: those with *any* media rules consume nearly 3 hours less media per day (2:52) than those with no rules."

(Rule Number One: No TV in the bedroom. Duh.)

It's challenging not only to monitor the amount of time kids spend using media, but how they use it as well. According to OnlineFamily.Norton.com, a monitoring system offered by Internet security company Semantec, 2009's top five search terms for children and teens were "YouTube," "Google," "Facebook," "sex," and "porn." Clearly, some of those seven hours using media are unsupervised.

Common sense ought to tell us that there will be cultural repercussions for allowing our kids to develop what can only be described as a media obsession. For example, the KFF study reveals roughly 75 percent of seventh to twelfth graders have a profile on a social networking site. Meanwhile, Junior Achievement's 7th annual teen ethics survey finds these social networking sites have become so central to teens' lifestyles that more than half (58 percent) "would consider their ability to access them during working hours when weighing a job offer from a potential employer."

Um kids…Google "time theft" and see what you get.

It's time for us to get over our shock that what is happening right before our eyes is, in fact, happening right before our eyes. Parents (read: we) must teach Generation M to incorporate media into a balanced, healthy, whole life.

But more than that, we must be vocal and ardent advocates of censorship.

That's right, I used the "C" word.

But I'm not talking about using the government to enforce standards about what may or may not constitute protected speech in American media. I'm talking about creating and enforcing standards for media consumption in our homes that reflect the values and virtues we are trying to instill in our children. I'm talking about protecting our children's innocence and wholesomeness, and refusing to allow the radical Left to exploit their optimism and integrity in the name of liberalism.

It would be great if American media were all wholesome and acceptable, or at least if we had better systems to manage the media monster that has taken residence in our homes. Parents Television Council, of which I am an Advisory Board member, has long advocated cable choice, which would bar cable providers from forcing consumers to accept networks that we prefer to avoid into our homes. Cable choice—already a technological possibility (and an easy one, really)—would let us pick the ten or twelve or fourteen stations we tend to watch with regularity (apparently most of us watch less than a dozen, though we all get hundreds foisted on us). We would then be able to pay for only what we want and use (what a concept!), and our consumer choices would "naturally select" to the trash heap of failure the outlets that spew garbage into the airwaves. Who says conservatives don't believe in Darwinism?

Parents and grandparents and aunties and uncles and babysitters and moms across the street all must become censors of media content, not only in our homes, but in places where we are faced with the intrusion of corrupting content. Don't like the sleazy show they're playing in the pizza place where you're paying to enjoy a family night out? Ask the management to turn it off. Boom. Censorship. You're a fascist. What now, Leftists? (Sorry. Channeling my teenagers.)

What's more, we cannot let the radical Left continue their monopoly of the media without objection. Object, and do it most fervently around your kitchen table, where your children and grandchildren will learn why you are offended by biased news coverage and bare-naked movie stars and radical environmentalists and activists of all kinds who seek to indoctrinate you and your loved ones. Visit Parentstv.org to learn more.

Restoring Civic Virtue

And finally, the only sure avenue to restore the next American generation: we must restore their virtue. Benjamin Franklin said, "Only a virtuous people are capable of freedom. As nations become corrupt and vicious, they have more need of masters." Samuel Adams wrote, "If Virtue & Knowledge are diffused among the People, they will never be enslav'd. This will be their great Security." And John Adams wrote, "If there is a form of government, then, whose principle and foundation is virtue, will not every sober man acknowledge it better calculated to promote the general happiness than any other form?"

The civic virtue of our Founders, themselves imperfect beings, still serves as the example and ideal for the development of moral citizenship in America today. Imbuing our children with virtues for personal conduct, public conduct, and civic leadership will restore America in the next generation. This is the key to revitalizing our republic, and to reigniting the love of freedom in the hearts of our youngest citizens.

Civic Virtues to Guide Personal Conduct

Self-discipline

Self-discipline is the foundation for building all virtue. When we teach young people the habits of self-discipline and self-control, they are able to acquire all sorts of admirable and honorable traits. Rather than buy into the pop culture myths about the necessity of teenage rebellion and the inevitability of childhood misbehavior, we can raise the bar of our expectations and assume this generation is capable of the same courage and dedication as generations past. We need to teach our children that liberty is a blessing, and that freedom and license are not the same. We must instill in them the capacity for mastery, which comes from self-discipline—for out of mastery comes achievement.

Forbearance

It's hard to imagine America's children practicing patience, much less the virtue of long-suffering. In a culture that believes temper tantrums are developmentally appropriate, and where lifelong immaturity results in road rage and necessitates anger management courses for adults, we see the consequences of living in a society where people put their wants even before the needs of others. Forbearance is the virtue that displays maturity. Our children must learn that, though life is not fair, the virtue of patience is freely available to every person. As parents, we must stop indulging our children's every wish and whim, smoothing the way so that they are never frustrated or denied. Instead, as the proverb says, we should "Prepare the child for the path, not the path for the child." From forbearance comes compassion, and from compassion comes the charity to build a nation of righteous citizens.

Humility

Our hyper-competitive American culture has allowed us to ignore the need for humility, yet this virtue is the basis for dignity and respect. The self-esteem obsession that has grown into a dangerous sense of narcissism among our youth is evident in their quest for fame and notoriety. As well, parents too often protect children from the gift of failure and the lessons that only disappointment can provide. Humility, which they must learn by living accountably for their actions, will permit our children to have genuine respect for others. Out of humility comes respect, and out of respect comes gratitude.

Moderation

In America, no thought goes unexpressed (but many should). We expose our dirty laundry on reality shows and Facebook pages and blogs, and we allow our children to believe that every urge and whim is permissible, natural, and appropriate. Our over-emotionalism, evident in all our public discourse, teaches our children that whoever has the loudest megaphone wins the debate. If we teach moderation in all things—from material possessions to emotional expressions, from the foods we consume to the time we spend entertaining ourselves—we will instill the virtue that underlies temperance and prudence and discernment.

Civic Virtues to Guide Public Conduct

Honor

America's Founders pledged and risked their "sacred honor" to forge our new nation. But the idea of honor as a virtue to be guarded for its inherent goodness is sadly lost in our current culture. Our children don't worry about their dignity or reputations as they should, because they too often see that there are few repercussions to losing the good esteem of others. And parents, so concerned with promoting their children's achievements, are sometimes willing to teach their children dishonorable habits to get ahead. Only when they feel the pain of shame can our children understand the value of honor. Yet we adults routinely protect our children from the consequences of their actions. If we teach our children the value of their good word, they will absorb the trait of integrity. From integrity comes honor, and from honor comes inspiration.

Civility

The call to greater civility is heard from the halls of Congress to the steps of the academy. Every media pundit and political player and talk radio jock in every blue and red state in the nation knows that civility in America has been lost and must be found again. Yet we continue to practice and model for our children habits of incivility that teach more than our hollow words will ever communicate. In fact, manners and etiquette are considered old-fashioned and outdated, while our casual culture (think rubber flip flops in the White House Rose Garden—sorry, Northwestern University Women's Lacrosse team) has overtaken our social norms. But there are reasons for etiquette and rules for civil discourse (Rule No. One: There are things you *just don't say*). Those rules offer a society structure. From etiquette comes civility, and from civility comes equanimity—the poise to remain composed in even the most fervent debate.

Independence

Nothing hurts our young people more than the sense that they are incapable of independence. Yet that's just the message being sent by the Left when it advocates for a prolonged adolescence and a so-called slow path to adulthood. Helicopter parents who follow their young adult children to college and into the workforce send the message that being a "grown-up" is optional and unnecessary. That assumption is exacerbated by government efforts to increase parental liability for what were previously adult responsibilities. Even in young childhood, we are hardwired to yearn for independence ("All by myself!"). Formerly, the goal of parenting was to render oneself obsolete. To instill the virtue of independence, we must cut our children free and allow them the satisfaction of forging lives for themselves. From self-reliance comes self-confidence, and from self-confidence comes independence.

Reason

The radical and atheist Left loves to invoke the "Age of Reason" as proof that our Founders were men of the Enlightenment. But reason and faithlessness are not one and the same. In fact, it's the hyper-emotionalism of the Left ("I feel your pain" and other trite pronouncements) that has eroded reason as the basis for argument and decision-making. With immature philosophies such as "follow your heart," we train our children to believe that creating a vision for their futures or establishing goals and aspirations is merely a matter of being in touch with their feelings. At the same time, we convince them that their self-image is incapable of surviving an insult. Thus in addition to being overly emotional, they're not particularly resilient. We must teach our children that it is noble to think, believe, and know things in our minds, not only to feel things in our hearts. When we convey to our children that passion is not a substitute for knowledge, we can instill the virtue of reason. From reason comes understanding, and from understanding comes persuasion.

Civic Virtues to Guide the Nation

Citizenship

If we are going to save our American republic, we must teach our children what it is. By dumbing down "democracy" and using that watered-down term to describe our unique and complex form of government, we have allowed the radical Left to hijack the vocabulary of liberty for their own illiberal purposes. As Ben Franklin famously said, it's "A Republic, if you can keep it." To raise up a generation of worthy citizens, we need to resurrect the ideals of citizenship—even the "Citizenship Award" of old. And we can no longer tolerate an educational system that permits ignorance and propaganda to inform the political identity of an entire generation. From informed citizenship comes effective participation and from effective participation comes true civic leadership.

Magnanimity

If our children's generation is to answer the call to greatness, we must raise the bar of our expectations. When we do this, we discover that our young people are ready, willing, and able to do hard things, purposeful things, and even self-sacrificial things. We have allowed our nation's children to become jaded and cynical. Shame on us for permitting their natural optimism and idealism to slink into apathy. Restoring America means rebuilding a sense of idealism in our children. From idealism will come magnanimity. From magnanimity, history is made.

Fidelity

Our children deserve more than simple platitudes about national pride. Bumper-sticker patriotism only highlights the contrast between those who complain and those who serve, while bastardizations of our heritage (Memorial Day Sales, anyone?) celebrate rampant consumerism rather than love for God and country. We must teach our children not the media version of heroism, but the heroic character ingrained in the people all around us. And we must accept and teach that our American citizenship requires us to define the hill on which we would die, rather than lose the liberty that affords our way of life. Faithfulness to America cannot be reserved for the few and the proud, but must be inherent in our children's character. For only from fidelity comes sacrifice, and in sacrifice is our security.

Reverence

Nothing indicts us as a generation of adults more than the unbelief of our children. That our youth are doubtful of God means they have been abandoned—not by God but by those whose obligation is to lead them to his service. In a country where nothing is sacred and everything is fodder for the amusement of cynics, and where reverence has long since been replaced by political correctness, we must return God to the public square and to the hearts and minds of our children. By instilling simple respect for the faithfulness that inspired our founding, we can recapture the reverence that caused our nation to be. From reverence comes blessedness, and the enduring promise that is America.

ACKNOWLEDGMENTS

Though writing appears to be a solitary pursuit, it's really quite a collaborative process. I'm grateful to everyone who helped me bring this book to fruition.

At Regnery Publishing, I am indebted to Publisher Marji Ross, Executive Editor Harry W. Crocker III, Managing Editor Mary Beth Baker, Art Director Amanda Larsen, Designer Amber Colleran, and elsewhere within Eagle Publishing to Jeffrey Carneal, Joe Guerriero, Maritza Lizama, Chris Pascuzzo, Tony Cane, and Adam Tragone. Special thanks to my editor, Elizabeth Kantor, for unburying the lead, challenging me to reconfigure chapters, and most of all for her patience and insight as she helped me improve my manuscript.

Every author needs a champion. Mine is Kathy Lubbers, to whom I cannot express adequate thanks. Her positive attitude and dogged determination to succeed are surpassed only by her warmth and loyalty. She is an extraordinary agent and an even lovelier friend.

Like all Americans, I'm surrounded by loved ones of various political stripes and I'm grateful to each of them for challenging and informing my perspective. Whether or not they agree with my opinions, they have supported and encouraged me throughout this project. Thank you to the Brennan, Campbell, Radelet, Bernard, and Kennedy families, and especially to my parents, Tom and Polly, and to Ellen and Catherine for calling even when the phone is on silent.

Thank you to dear friends Theresa Foote and Jackie Cushman, and to the wonderful staff of St. Francis Retreat Center in Dewitt, Michigan, my home away from home.

My heartfelt thanks go to my incredible husband, Jim, whose stalwart belief in my abilities is most certainly unfounded and a reflection of his unwavering devotion; and to our four amazing children: Kate, Betsy, Jimmy, and Amy. Your love, patience, and inspiration kept me going during the most difficult days of this effort. I hope you're as proud of me as I am of you.

Finally, feebly, I thank God Almighty for the privilege of living in the most beautiful and bountiful nation on earth, and for the freedom to express my love for him and the country I am blessed to call home.

Marybeth Hicks
June 2011
East Lansing, Michigan

INDEX